# A Victorian Guide to Birmingham

In 1838, when the railway arrived in Birmingham, it was the first major town in England to have a direct line to London. The town, ('city' status wasn't granted until 1889) had grown rapidly over the previous century, was Britain's second largest conurbation and at the centre of its industrial heartland. As such, there was good economic reason to connect it to the nation's capital by the latest and fastest mode of transport. The railway network continued to expand and by the 1890s, Birmingham was within easy reach of many towns and villages. Visitors flocked to the city in ever-increasing numbers for business, shopping and entertainment and to enjoy its impressive buildings, public spaces and grand arcades. On arrival, they wanted to know where to go and what to see and guide-books were published to help them make the most of their trip.

This book combines text from a Birmingham guide printed in 1894 and thirty photographs from 'magic lantern' projection slides dating from the late-nineteenth and early-twentieth centuries.

The guide-book is remarkably detailed with information on hotels; restaurants; horse-drawn cabs, trams and omnibuses; public baths etc. but perhaps more importantly from an historical perspective, over half of it is devoted to three guided walks, pointing out places and buildings of interest and explaining their purpose and history. In addition, there are sections on parks, public institutions and the city's industries.

The photographs are from a different source. They were taken by professional photographers to be used as projection slides, to entertain and inform audiences in shows and talks.

The text and photographs complement each other and enable us to travel back in time to this important Victorian city.

*Andrew Gill*

THE MIDLAND INSTITUTE.

# GUIDE TO BIRMINGHAM.

## INTRODUCTION.

IN the following pages, we describe the distinguishing features of Birmingham—"the metropolis of the Midlands," as it is called—a city which has advanced during the past hundred years, by leaps and bounds, from the status of a third-rate town to that of the fourth city of the empire, and the progress whereof, socially, commercially, and politically, has excited the admiration of all who have witnessed it. We treat of its history, at sufficient length, in our first Chapter; and as we walk through the streets of the city, we shall see that the architecture of its numerous public buildings is quite "up to date"—in advance, indeed, of that of many of the large towns in "this England of ours." Here, therefore, we need only note that it is for its manufactures that the place is famous; and that though, as a rule, holiday-makers shun everything that savours of business and reminds them of their work-a-day avocations, yet so numerous and interesting are the processes and so wonderful the machinery employed in Birmingham's many industries that few tourists through the pleasant and famous tract of country by which the city is surrounded fail in paying a visit to "Europe's grand toyshop," the more especially as its principal factories are thrown open to their inspection on any day, except Saturday. Elsewhere, we devote several pages to an enumeration of the chief features of Birmingham's commercial activity; in this introductory Chapter, therefore, we will briefly notice the provision made for the comfort and well-being of her visitors—and her residents, too, to a great extent. The first thing a visitor to any town refers to is the position and character of—

## The Hotels,

in which he and his friends may find that "warmest welcome" for which the disciples of St. Boniface have ever been noted. Though, at the end of the eighteenth century, Birmingham only possessed one hotel, worthy of the name, the *Royal*—now one of the chief restaurants in the city—the city is now well supplied with good "houses of entertainment" of all kinds. Their tariffs, as will be seen from the following list, are not unreasonable. The figures were in every case furnished by the proprietors of the principal hotels; but as there are times when beds are in such request that it is only reasonable to expect that higher prices will be asked, and as, like every other undertaking, they do at times pass "under entirely new management," it would be well to verify them by correspondence, before sending one's "traps" to any particular house:—

[ABBREVIATIONS: *R.*, bedrooms; *B.*, breakfast; *L.*, luncheon; *D.*, dinner; *T.*, tea; *A.*, attendance; *fr.*, from; *temp.*, temperance.]

**Grand**, Colmore Row: *R.*, 2/- to 4/-; *B.* or *T.*, 1/- to 3/-; *L.*, 1/- to 3/-—*table d'hôte*, 3/6; *D.* (*table d'hôte*), 5/-; *A.*, 1/6.
*Pension* (for not less than seven days), 10/6 per day.

**Great Western**, Colmore Row: *R.*, 3/- to 5/-; *B.*, 2/6 to 3/-; *L.*, 2/- to 2/6; *D.* (*table d'hôte*), 4/6; *T.*, 1/6 to 2/6; *A.*, 1/6.
*Pension*, 12/- per day, or 73/6 per week.

**Midland**, New Street: *R.*, *fr.* 2/-; *B.* or *T.* *fr.* 2/-; *L.* *fr.* 2/6; *D.* *fr.* 3/6; *A.*, 1/6.
*Pension*, 10/6 per day, or 63/- per week.

**Colonnade**, New Street: *B.* and *A.*, 3/6; *B.* or *D.*, 2/6; *L.* or *T.*, 2/-.
*Pension*, 8/6 per day.

**Queen's and North-Western**, New Street Station.

**Cobden**, Corporation Street (*temp.*): *R.* and *A.*, 2/6; *B.*, *L.*, or *T.*, 1/- to 2/-; *D.*, 2/-, or *à la carte*, One of the finest Temperance Hotels in the kingdom.

**Victoria**, Corporation Street: *R.* and *A.*, 3/- (two persons, 4/-); *B.*, *L.*, or *T.*, 2/-; *D.*, 2/6; plain tea, 1/-.

**Central** (*temp.*), Temple Street: *R.* and *A.*, 2/-; *B.* or *T.*, 1/- to 1/9.

**Clarke's** (*temp.*), Moor Street:

**Belgrave**, Moseley Road:

**Bullivant's**, Carr's Lane:

**Dingley's**, Moor Street:

**Knapp's**, High Street:

**Lee's**, Livery Street (*temp.*): *R.*, 1/6; *B.* or *T.*, 1/6; *L.* or *D.*, "according to order"; *A.*, -/6.
*Pension*, 4/6 per day (two meals only).

**Market**, near New Street Railway Station: *R.* and *A.*, 2/-; *B.* or *T.*, 1/- to 1/9; *L.* or *D.*, 1/6.
*Pension*, 6/6 per day, or 42/- per week.

**Plough and Harrow**, Hagley Road: *R.* and *A.*, 4/- to 5/-; *B.* or *L.*, 2/6; *D.*, 3/6; *T.*, *fr.* 1/-.
*Pension*, 63/- to 84/- per week.

**Stork**, Corporation Street:

**Swan**, New Street:

**White Horse**, Congreve Street: *R.* and *A.*, 2/6; *B.* or *T.*, 2/-; *L* (*table d'hôte*), 1/6; *D.* (*table d'hôte*), 2/6.

**Waverley**, New Meeting Street: *R.* and *A.*, 1/6 to 2/6; *B.* or *T.*, 1/- to 2/-; *L.*, 1/6.

**Wilkins's** (*temp.*), Moor Street: *R.* and *A.*, 2/-; *B.* or *T.*, 1/- to 2/-; *D.* *fr.* 1/6.

**Woolpack**, Moor Street: *R.*, 2/6; *B.* or *T.*, 2/- to 2/6; *L.*, 2/6; *D.* "as ordered"; *A.*, 1/-.

## Restaurants,

proper, are plentiful in the city; they are attached, moreover, to most of the hotels. The following are among the chief (the information as to prices, &c., may be relied upon):—

Grand Hotel: *Table d'hôte* luncheon, 12.30 to 3 p.m., 2/6 and 3/6; *table d'hôte* dinner, 6 to 8 p.m., 5/-; *à la carte*, at all times.

Ye Olde Royal, Temple Row:

Queen's Hotel: Luncheons, 2/- and 2/6; dinners, from 2/6 to 4/-; special dinners, from 5/-.

Great Western Hotel: *Table d'hôte*, 6 to 7.30 p.m., 4/-; hot luncheon, 2/6.

Midland Hotel: Hot luncheon, 1 to 3 p.m., 2/6; *table d'hôte*, 6 to 8 p.m., 4/-.

Swan Hotel: Dinner at 1.15.

Colonnade Hotel: *Table d'hôte*, from 12 to 3 p.m.

Stork Hotel: *Table d'hôte* dinner, 1.15 p.m., 2/6; cold luncheon, 2/-.

Cobden, Temperance Hotel: Dinner *à la carte*, from 1.0 to 2.30 p.m.

Lisseter and Miller's Restaurant, Bennett's Hill: Dinners *à la carte*, from 12.30 to 4 p.m.

Café Royal, 62, New Street: Luncheons and dinners, from 12.30 to 4.0 p.m.

Pattison's Restaurants, 7, New Street, 54. High Street, and Corporation Street.

Birmingham Restaurant, 101, New Street: Dinners *à la carte*, from 12 to 3 p.m.; tea and coffee, at all hours.

Nock's Restaurant, Union Passage, connecting New Street and Corporation Street: Cold luncheons, soups, chops, &c., from 10 a.m.; dinners, from 12 to 3 p.m.; teas, suppers, &c., till 11 p.m.

Birmingham Dairy Company, Limited, Temperance Restaurant, New Street and Corporation Street.

Garden Restaurant, Paradise Street: Vegetarian.

Birmingham School of Cookery, Restaurant, Colmore Row.

Market Hotel, Station Street: *Table d'hôte*, 1.0 to 2.30, 1/6; cold snacks, &c.

## Places of Worship.

It goes without saying that a city of the size of Birmingham is well supplied with churches and chapels, belonging to all the varied denominations into which Christendom is divided; the Jews, moreover, have a synagogue in the place. "What time does the service at such-and-such a church (or chapel) commence to-day?"

is a frequent question from a visitor to the host or waiter at an hotel; and as it often happens that the person addressed has never heard of the particular sanctuary referred to, the "stranger within the gates" has considerable difficulty in obtaining the information desired and perhaps does not reach his destination till the service is nearly half over. To save our readers from similar trouble and disappointment — and because we consider that no Guide can be complete without it—we give, in Appendix A, a complete list of the places of worship in Birmingham, with the hours of service at each, corrected up to the latest date.

## Cab Fares.

These are arranged by the authorities as under:—

Hansoms, -/8 per mile (with minimum fare of 1/-); 2/6 per hour. Four wheelers, 1/- per mile; 3/- per hour.

## Tramcars, Omnibuses, &c.

Omnibuses start—
 From opposite King Edward's School, New Street, for Broad Street, Five Ways, and various parts of Edgbaston, *via* Hagley Road, Harborne Road, Calthorpe Road, and Pershore Road.
 From High Street for Shirley, Yardley, Hay Mills, Sheldon, and Bordesley Green.

Tramcars start—
 From Suffolk Street, for Bristol Road, Bournbrook, and Selly Oak.
 ,, John Bright Street, for Balsall Heath, Moseley, King's Heath, Small Heath, and Sparkbrook.
 ,, Albert Street, Dale End, for Bloomsbury and Nechells.
 ,, Old Square, for Aston, Gravelly Hill, Erdington, Saltley, Witton, and Perry Barr.
 ,, Great Western Hotel, Colmore Row, for Hockley and Handsworth.
 ,, Lionel Street, Summer Row, for Winson Green, Smethwick, Oldbury, West Bromwich, and Dudley.

## Baths.

The **Corporation Baths**, Kent Street, comprise first and second class swimming, hot and cold private, and Turkish baths. The swimming and private baths are open, during week days, from

7.0 a.m. till 8.0 p.m. (Saturdays, till 9.0 p.m.). The first-class swimming bath is reserved for ladies on Wednesday evenings, from 7.0 p.m., and on Saturday mornings, from 10.0 to 12.0.

The **Corporation Baths,** Monument Road, fifteen minutes from the principal parts of Edgbaston, contain the same accommodation as Kent Street, and are open during the same hours.

There are also **Corporation Baths** in Woodcock Street and Northwood Street.

**Private Turkish Baths,** Broad Street and High Street (for gentlemen only). Open daily (except Sunday) from 8.0 a.m. to 9.0 p.m. Single ticket, 2/6; five persons, 11/-; ten, 20/-. After 7.0 p.m., 2/-. Plunge or shower bath, without shampooing, 1/-.

THE POST OFFICE.

**Birmingham Council House**

**The Bull Ring**

Alum Rock Road, Saltley

The Assembly Rooms, Edgbaston

**Birmingham University Lecture Hall used as a Red Cross Hospital during the First World War**

The Boating Lake, Cannon Hill Park

**Broad Street from Five Ways**

**Broad Street**

**Broad Street**

**The Bull Ring**

**Bull Street**

Cannon Hill Park

**City Arcade**

Colmore Row

**Corporation Street**

**Corporation Street**

**Birmingham Fire Brigade**

**Birmingham Fire Brigade**

**Great Western Arcade**

Hagley Road

High Street

The last horse tram, Nechells, 30th September 1906

**The Market Hall**

Matthews' Grocery Store, Aston

**New Street Station**

**New Street Station**

**New Street**

Perry Bar

Snow Hill Station

Victoria Road, Aston

**Winson Green Road**

NEW STREET RAILWAY STATION.

# BIRMINGHAM: ITS GEOGRAPHICAL POSITION, HISTORY, &c.

"Illustrious offspring of Vulcanic toil!
Pride of the country! Glory of the isle!
Europe's grand toy-shop! Art's exhaustless mine!
These and more titles, Birmingham, are thine."

BIRMINGHAM ARMS.

BIRMINGHAM, the metropolis of the Midland Counties of England, lies on the north-western border of Warwickshire, its suburbs spreading into the adjacent counties of Stafford and Worcester. It was originally built on an undulating site on the banks of the small river Rea, which flows into the Tame, a tributary of the Trent; but that stream now traverses but a small portion of its area. Geographically speaking, the town is situated in latitude 52° 29" N. and longitude 1° 48" W.;

39

it is 109 miles from London,* 82 from Manchester, 90 from Liverpool, 20 from Warwick, 23½ from Leamington, 26 from Stratford, 18 from Coventry, and 12½ from Wolverhampton. The city is well supplied with railways, the North-Western, Great Western, and Midland systems having main arteries through it and sending out branches to all the neighbouring towns; and report has it that another large company is turning its attention to the desirability of sharing in its enormous traffic. Several of the great high roads of Great Britain, too, converge at this spot; and the want of a navigable river, in which respect it differs from nearly every other large town in the United Kingdom, is supplied by an extensive system of canals, which connect it with all the principal rivers of England and enabled the town to "make each port around the coast her own," long before the railways carried away her manufactures at the rate which they now do. Birmingham ranks as the fourth largest city in the United Kingdom; and in 1894 there were, within the limits of the city, 95,516 houses and a population of 487,897.

Referring to the name of the town, we are told by Mr. Hamper, a local antiquarian, that "the four last centuries have produced eight modes of presenting it to our eye, and of ringing as many changes upon our ear; exclusive of upwards of one hundred different ways of spelling it." These "eight modes" are *Brumwychcham*, *Bermyngeham*, *Bromwycham*, *Burmyngham*, *Bermyngham*, *Byrmyngham*, *Bromicham*, and *Birmingham*. We may, perhaps, be permitted to add to them the word *Brummagem* (obviously, a coarse pronunciation of Bromwycham), commonly applied to the mock jewellery, at one time so extensively manufactured in the town, and *Bremicham*, the spelling of Camden.

While the orthography of the name has been subject to so many changes, its derivation has given rise to no

* This is the geographical distance. By North-Western Railway it is 113, and by Great Western 128 miles.

small amount of controversy. Writers on the subject may be divided into three schools—those claiming a British, a Roman, and a Saxon origin for the town. Among the former, was Hutton, the historian, who carried his theory to such an extent as to assert that the early British settlement consisted of eighty houses, inhabited by four hundred souls. While thinking the name "too remote for certain explanation," he says it "seems to have been *Bromwich*—'brom,' perhaps from the broom, or shrub, for the growth of which the soil is extremely favourable ; *wych*, 'a descent'—this exactly corresponds with the declivity from the High Street to Digbeth"; while *ham*, Saxon for "home," was probably, he thinks, added many centuries after, when "a series of prosperity attending it, its lord might assume its name and reside in it." Other writers of this school have traced the name to *bremden*, "the high stone," or *bryngwyan*, "the white mount." Those who contend for a Roman origin for the town point to the proximity of Watling Street and to the fact that Icknield Street passes through its suburbs, and aver that *Bremænium* stood on the spot and give its name to the place. Among them, was Hamper, who has written at length on the subject. While the advocates of the Saxon derivation of the name—among whom was Dugdale—agree with Hutton in saying the town was originally called *Bromwycham*, they contend that it was derived from the *Broommings* or *Brummings* (sons of Berms), a Saxon tribe who settled there in early days, and *ham*, "a home."

But leaving those learned in such matters to fight over and over again the battle as to the derivation and original spelling of the name, we have indisputable evidence that, in early Saxon times, the town was called *Brumwychcham*, an unmusical and uncouth word, which, when William the Norman conquered the kingdom, had been softened into something like its present form. In Domesday Book, we find it spelt *Bermingeham* :—

"Richard holds of William [Fitz-Ausculf] four hides in Bermingeha'. The arable employs six ploughs ; one is in the demesne.

BIRMINGHAM, FROM THE SOUTH.

There are five villeins and four borders, with two ploughs. Wood half a mile long and two furlongs broad. It was and is worth twenty shillings."

So that the place had escaped the troubles which, at that most momentous epoch of our history, reduced so many thriving towns and villages in size and value. Probably, this immunity from the calamities which overtook their brethren in other parts of the land may be attributed to the fact that the inhabitants had even then developed the art of attending exclusively to their own petty interests and letting alone the greater affairs of state and politics which distinguished them till quite modern days.

We know but little of the Birmingham of those early days. Though in all probability scarcely deserving the name of village in the modern acceptation of the term, it must have been a place of note; for we find that, a few years later, the lord of the manor considered it of sufficient importance to adopt its name. "Peter de Bermingham," says Hutton, "had a castle here, and lived here in splendour." Dugdale tells us that this castle " stood scarce a bowshot from the church south-westward ; " and modern investigation has established the fact that its site is occupied by the Smithfield of to-day, Moat Row and Moat Lane indicating the position of the ditch around it, which still existed in Hutton's time. Peter's descendants followed his example, dwelling in the castle for some four hundred years; until, in the reign of Henry VIII., the ambitious Dudley, Duke of Northumland, who coveted the property, succeeded in ousting Edward, the last of the family. But he did not live at the old castle, although the estates, which were forfeited to the crown, were conferred on him; and it does not appear that it was ever again occupied. At any rate, it fell into decay; and has long since disappeared. Edward lost the estates in 1537; and Leland, who visited Birmingham in the following year, gives us an account of the town. From this, it would appear that, even at that early date, the inhabitants had begun to develop that genius for manufacture which has made Birmingham what it is. He says:—

"I came through a praty street, or ever I entred into Berming-ham towne. This street, as I remember, is called Dirtey. In it, dwell smithes and cutlers, and there is a brook that divideth this street from Bermingham, and is a Hamlett, or Member, belonginge to the Parish Thereby. There is at the end of Dirtey a propper chappell, and mansion house of tymber, hard on the ripe [bank], as the brooke runneth downe; and as I went through the ford by the bridge, the water downe on the right hand, and a few miles lower goeth into Tame, ripa dextra. This brooke, above Dirtey, breaketh in two armes, that, a little beneath the bridge, close again. This brooke riseth, as some say, four or five miles above Bermingham, toward Black Hilles. The beauty of Bermingham, a goode markett towne in the extreme parts of Warwickshire, is one street going up a longe, almost from the left ripe of the brooke, up a meane hill by the length of a quarter of a mile. I saw but one Parroch Church in the towne. There be many smithes in the towne that use to make knives and all manner of cuttinge tooles, and many loriners that make bittes, and a great many naylors. Soe that a great part of the towne is maintained by smithes, who have their iron and sea-cole out of Staffordshire."

The "Dirtey" of Leland is the Deritend of to-day, and its "propper chapell" and "mansion house of tymber" are both still in existence; the latter is the **Old Crown House,** with a representation of which we present our readers.

Camden, who visited Birmingham between 1576 and 1586, has left us an interesting record of what he thought of the town. He says:—

"*Bremicham,* full of inhabitants, and resounding with hammers and anvils, for the most of them are smiths. The lower part thereof standeth very waterish; the upper riseth with faire buildings: for the credit and praise whereof, I may not reckon this, in the last place, that the noble and martiall family of the *Bremichams,* Earles of *Louth,* &c., in Ireland, fetched their originall and name from hence."

During the centuries which intervened between the Norman Conquest and the Civil War of 1641, the people of Birmingham stood aloof from domestic broils and quietly minded their own business; hence, their prosperous condition. There was, however, one exception to this rule, and that was on the occasion of the battle of

Evesham in Henry III.'s reign, when they sent forth a body of men to fight on the side of the barons and of liberty. At the outbreak of the war between Charles I. and his Parliament, Birmingham zealously espoused the Roundhead cause, supplied the Parliamentary troops with arms, and seized the royal plate and furniture which the king left, when passing through the town on his way from Shrewsbury to London. The burgesses suffered severely for their spirited action. No doubt sympathising with Clarendon in his denunciation of the town, as "declaring more personal malice against his Majesty than any other place," Prince Rupert resolved on an exemplary revenge; and, in the following April, attacked the town at the head of two thousand men, plundered it, and set it on fire in several places, the Earl of Denbigh, one of the Royalist leaders, being slain in the fight. These were the only occasions on which, till the commencement of the nineteenth century, the town took any part in the politics of the nation. Indeed, with the exception of a severe outbreak of the plague in 1665 (the same year in which London was so grievously afflicted), no noteworthy event occurred in the history of Birmingham till 1791, when the oft-told Priestley riots occurred. In 1832, the Political Union of Birmingham exercised considerable influence in effecting the passage of the Reform Bill. From this measure, the town first obtained the privilege of representation in Parliament. The Representation of the People Act of 1866 gave Birmingham a third member; and the Redistribution Act of 1885 increased the number of its representatives to seven and divided the parliamentary borough into seven parts, allowing a single member to each. Birmingham was made an assize town in 1884; and it received a royal charter, constituting it a city, in the year 1889. The access of dignity gave it the privilege of adding supporters and a crest to its coat of arms. The latter is officially described as consisting of—

"A wreath of colours and a mural crown, issuent therefrom a dexter arm, *embowered*, the hand holding a hammer (*all proper*)."

The supporters are :—

"On the dexter side, a man, habited as a smith (representing industry), holding in the dexter hand a hammer, resting on an anvil (*all proper*); and on the sinister side, a female figure (representing art) (*proper, vested argand*), wreathed round the temples with laurel (*vert*), tied by a ribbon (*gules*), holding, in the dexter hand, resting on the shield, a book bound (*also gules*), and in the sinister, a painter's palette (*or*), with two brushes (*proper*)."

The motto is, "Forward".

In 1891, the city was extended, so as to include Balsall Heath, Harborne, and Saltley; and the boundaries of the counties hereabouts were so readjusted that the whole of Birmingham is now included in Warwickshire.

The city possesses a court of quarter sessions of its own, presided over by a recorder; and it is governed by a corporation, consisting of a mayor and one alderman and three councillors for each of its eighteen wards. Educational matters are managed by a School Board, established in the November after the passing of the Elementary Education Act. It consists of fifteen members, and has done good work in promoting the spread of education. Aston, one of Birmingham's suburbs, possesses a separate school board, consisting of thirteen members, and a local board, and includes a population of eighty thousand persons.

As an indication of the progressive rise of Birmingham to its present dimensions, we append a return, tabulated from Hutton's "History of Birmingham" and the census returns. Hutton's figures extend to 1780, and we need scarcely say that many of them are mere conjectures; the others of course can be relied upon :—

|  | Houses. | Persons. |  | Houses. | Persons. |
|---|---|---|---|---|---|
| In the days of the Ancient Britons | 80 | 400 | In 1801 | 15,650 | 73,670 |
| In 750 | 600 | 3,000 | In 1811 | 16,096 | 85,755 |
| In 1066 | 700 | 3,500 | In 1821 | 21,345 | 106,722 |
| In 1650 | 900 | 5,472 | In 1831 | 29,397 | 146,986 |
| In 1700 | 2,504 | 15,032 | In 1841 | 40,000 | 182,922 |
| In 1731 | 3,717 | 23,286 | In 1851 | 48,894 | 232,841 |
| In 1741 | 4,114 | 24,660 | In 1861 | 59,200 | 295,955 |
| In 1781 | 8,382 | 50,295 | In 1871 | 74,416 | 343,000 |
| In 1791 | 12,681 | 73,653 | In 1881 | 78,379 | 400,757 |
|  |  |  | In 1891 | 85,624 | 478,117 |

These figures, it must be recollected, refer only to Birmingham itself, without any reference to the miles of suburban streets which radiate in every direction, and which form to all intents and purposes a part of the city.

We have already noticed the fact that, up till 1832, Birmingham took little or no interest in politics. But when its inhabitants did wake up to their duty as citizens of that empire on which the sun never sets, they threw themselves into the troubled waters with the energy which they display in everything else. They have made their mark on our national institutions. The passage of the Reform Act was, as we have seen, materially accelerated by their action; and in more recent days, the city has been the head-quarters of the patriotic Liberal-Unionist party.

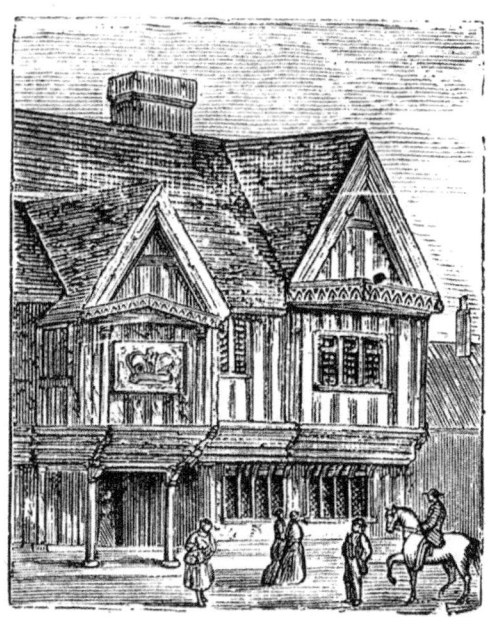

THE OLD CROWN HOUSE.

CHAMBERLAIN SQUARE.

THE QUEEN'S COLLEGE.

## WALKS ABOUT BIRMINGHAM.

STATUE OF PRIESTLEY.

BIRMINGHAM'S public buildings are modern and handsome—just the kind we should expect to meet with in a city that has made the rapid progress which she has; for it is a matter of regret that, under such circumstances, the edifices to which old age has imparted interest disappear rapidly before the requirements of commerce. The most convenient way of making one's acquaintance with the architectural features of any town is to walk through its streets and note them as they present them-

THE TOWN HALL.

selves to our view; and in Birmingham this plan is more than usually easy of adoption. For its public edifices are, for the most part, to be found in the triangle of splendid streets which form the centre of the modern town, one corner of which touches St. Martin's Church, and in the line of thoroughfares which extends from the New Street railway station to Aston. This has been opened out by the construction of wide and handsome Corporation Street, the most recent addition to the avenues of the city proper, and one which would hold its own in a competition with the chief street of any city in the empire—not excepting Regent Street, in the metropolis, or Princes Street, in the capital of the north. We will, therefore, first conduct our readers on an imaginary walk through the streets referred to, and afterwards notice such edifices of note as we do not meet in our trips, and visit the various suburbs of the town. Let us commence our journey at a nook (one of the many formed here and there by the irregularity of the streets) which may be properly called—

## THE HEART OF BIRMINGHAM.

And a splendid heart it is ! Before us is—

### The Town Hall,

said to be "the most symmetrical and classical building in England;" while large and beautiful edifices stand at every angle of the open space on which we gaze. The Town Hall occupies a commanding position at the junction of New, Paradise, and Congreve Streets, and Colmore Row, and is in every way worthy of its site. Designed on the model of a Greek temple, with a foundation of rustic masonry, arcaded throughout, its outline is that of an oblong parallelogram, with eight columns at either end and thirteen at each side. The ceiling of the great hall is supported by Corinthian pilasters, with Decorated capitals and cornice; and the room is capable of holding seven thousand persons (standing). At one end, is the famous organ, by Hill, containing four thousand pipes, acted on by four beds of keys used at the celebrated triennial musical festivals, held in the hall on behalf of the funds of the General

Hospital. That of 1846 is memorable in the history of music because it was the occasion on which the oratorio, "Elijah," was introduced to the world, under the bâton of its composer, Mendelssohn, a bust of whom is one of the chief ornaments of the room. Mona marble is the material used in the construction of the hall, which was not completed until 1850, although it was opened to the public some sixteen years before that date.

Immediately opposite the Town Hall, at the corner of Paradise and Hill Streets, is—

### The Old Post Office,

a building of bold classical design, opened on the 28th of September, 1873. It is chiefly constructed of slabs of Bath stone, which rest upon immense blocks of Cornish granite, and is quite worthy of the site on which it stands. When the office was opened, it was hoped that it would be amply sufficient for the requirements of the postal and telegraphic service for a long time; but the business increased so rapidly that, in a comparatively short period, the authorities were compelled to make arrangements for an addition to it, and the foundation stone of—

### The New Post Office

was laid by the then Postmaster-General (Mr. Raikes) in March, 1889. It adjoins the old edifice, and stands to the east of the other on a square plot of land between Hill Street (which separates it from its elder brother) and Pinfold Street. Though the appearance of the latter is attractive, that of the new edifice completely eclipses it. It is in the French Renaissance style of architecture, with features of that of Queen Anne, and is upwards of eighty feet high. The principal entrance is in Paradise Street, and the letter boxes are in the Pinfold Street front. The large room is ornamented by a **Statue of Sir Rowland Hill**, the author of our present postal system—at one time, a resident in the neighbourhood. Constructed of Sicilian marble, it is from the chisel of Mr. Peter Hollins, a local artist, and was the result of a public subscription; it was removed from the Old Post Office to its present position in 1869.

The office is open to the public on week-days from 7.0 a.m. until 10.0 p.m.; on Sundays, from 7.0 to 10.0 a.m. only.

Mails leave frequently during the day, and letters for the London night mail may be posted up to 12.20 a.m., or till 12.30 with an extra half-penny stamp.

There are branch offices and wall and pillar boxes (the latter of which are locally known as "stumps") in all parts of the town.

The deliveries commence at 7.0, 9.30, and 11.30 a.m., and 1.45, 4.15, and 6.15 p.m.

Money order, savings bank, insurance, and annuity business is transacted between 10.0 a.m. and 5.0 p.m., and on Saturdays till 1.0 p.m.

The **Head Telegraph Office** is open continually, day and night; and it "goes without saying" that there are branch offices all over the city which are, as a rule, open from 8.0 a.m. till 8.0 p.m. on week-days.

The eastern side of the open space, formed by the junction of New Street and Colmore Row, is occupied by—

## Christ Church.

[Hours of service on Sundays—11.0 a.m., 3.0 p.m. (for men only), and 6.30 p.m. Hymnal Companion.]

It is a stone edifice of Roman-Doric architecture, the chief feature of whose front (the western end) is a tetra-style Doric portico, the pediment whereof is supported by four columns. It is usually known as the Free Church; and it owes its origin to a legacy of £500, left by Mr. Hawkins, of Burton-on-Trent, for its erection. An Act of Parliament, authorising the step, was passed in the following year; and the scheme was warmly supported by the inhabitants and others. Mr. W. P. Inge presented the site; the Bishop of Lichfield and Coventry attached the prebendary of Tachbrook in the Lichfield Cathedral to the living; and the king, George III., subscribed £1,000 to the fund and offered to lay the foundation stone in person. This he was prevented by illness from doing; but he sent the Earl of Dartmouth to represent him, and the stone was laid by the high bailiff (Birmingham at that time had no mayor), in his

Majesty's name, in 1803. The building is considered one of the ugliest in the town; and its appearance is not

THE MUNICIPAL BUILDINGS.

improved by the spire, out of keeping with the rest of the building, added in 1815, instead of a dome and cupola, which appeared in the design of the architect.

The custom of separating the sexes was formerly observed at this church, and this gave rise to the following smart epigram :—

"The churches in general we everywhere find
Are places where men to the women are joined :
But at Christ Church, it seems, they are more cruel-hearted,
For men and their wives are brought here to be parted."

To the north of Christ Church, its beautiful front forming a splendid commencement to the street architecture of Colmore Row, is—

## The Council House,

the first stone whereof was laid on June 17, 1874, by the Right Hon. J. Chamberlain, M.P., then mayor of the borough. It is a noble edifice of Corinthian architecture, in harmony with the Town Hall, which it so nearly adjoins. Its façades are richly ornamented with sculpture and mosaics, the chief design representing "Britannia rewarding the Birmingham Manufacturers." It is pointed in Derbyshire stone. As its name indicates, it contains accommodation for the officials of the corporation and a noble Council Chamber, with mayor's parlour, banqueting room, and reception rooms. At the entrance to the latter, are Woolner's **Statue of Queen Victoria** and Foley's **Statue of the Prince Consort** (the latter declared one of the eminent sculptor's most successful works). *The building is generally open to visitors between ten in the morning and four in the afternoon.*

## The City Art Gallery and Museum,

with a lofty clock tower, erected at a cost of nearly eight thousand pounds, stands at the back of the Council House. Its entrance faces Chamberlain Square. The Art Gallery is the most important in the provinces; it consists of an unrivalled collection of modern pictures by leading English artists, including Burne-Jones' celebrated work, "The Star of Bethlehem," Holman Hunt's "Two Gentlemen of Verona," Sir John Millais' "Blind Girl," Watt's "Roman Lady," Fred. Walker's "Old Gate," Ford Madox Brown's "Last of England," "Beata

Beatrix" by Dante Gabriel Rossetti, Albert Moore's "Dreamers," together with the most important collection of works by David Cox in existence, presented by the late Mr. Joseph Nettlefold.

The Museum consists of large collections of jewellery, gold and silversmiths' work; enamels (Limoges and Oriental); ivory carvings; Oriental porcelain, bronzes, and lacquer; European porcelain and earthenware; glass, decorative ironwork, steel work; carvings in wood, marble, and stone; textile fabrics; specimens of Italian art, comprising sculpture, woodwork, decorative ironwork, bronzes, majolica, metal work, glass, &c.; arms and armour of all ages and countries; Wedgwood ware, &c. In its rotunda, too, is Bruce Joy's **Statue of John Bright**. In the Gallery, moreover, are **Busts of David Cox**, the famous landscape painter, **William Scholefield**, at one time a representative of Birmingham in the House of Commons, and **Matthew Davenport Hill, Q.C.**, a former recorder of the borough.

*The Art Gallery is open on Monday, Tuesday, Thursday, and Saturday throughout the year, from ten till nine; on Wednesday and Friday, during the winter season (from October 1st to March 15th), from ten till four; during the summer (from March 16th to September 30th), from ten till six; on Sunday, throughout the year, from two till five. On all occasions, admission is free.* Special Loan Exhibitions are arranged from time to time; one of them was attended in three months by two hundred and sixty-eight thousand people. *A special feature is made of the cheap catalogues, which command an enormous sale.*

The centre of the open space in front of the Council House is ornamented by a colossal bronze **Statue of Sir Robert Peel**, standing on a pedestal of Portland granite; the entire height of the statue, including the pedestal, is nearly twenty-five feet. Unveiled in 1854, it was designed by Mr. Peter Hollins, and cast by Messrs. Elkington and Mason.

Not far from it, is a **Statue of Priestley**, erected in

1874, by the inhabitants of Birmingham, as an acknowledgment of the merits of the discoverer of oxygen, who was driven from the town by a mob in 1791. It is of white marble, and represents the "father of pneumatic chemistry" in the act of making his grand discovery; a lens is in one hand, and a vessel containing mercury in the other. It stands on a pedestal of Portland stone.

Nearer the Council House, is a white marble **Statue of J. S. Wright, M.P.**, a local politician and philanthropist, who died at a meeting in the Council House in 1880. The monument was the result of a public subscription. Unveiled in 1883, by Mr. John Bright, M.P., it is of heroic size, measuring nine feet and a half in height, and is mounted upon a pedestal of Portland stone, eleven feet high, of similar design to that of the Priestley statue.

Turning northwards, between the Council House and the Town Hall, we soon reach—

## Chamberlain Square,

an oasis at the back of the latter edifice. It is brightened by two circular beds of flowers, and is enclosed by low walls. Here, resting on asphalted walks, are some more memorials. In the centre of the square, and giving it its name is a **Monument to Joseph Chamberlain**, inaugurated in October, 1880, in the presence of that gentleman, then the junior M.P. for the borough and a member of Mr. Gladstone's second administration. It consists of an elaborately-carved drinking fountain of Gothic design, by Mr. J. H. Chamberlain, surmounted by an octagonal spire, rising to a height of sixty-five feet. Under one of the main niches, there is a medallion of Mr. Chamberlain (executed in relief by Mr. Thomas Woolner, R.A.), with a lengthy inscription, recording the early public services of the right hon. gentleman. To its right, is a **Statue of George Dawson**, composed of Sicilian marble; it is a little larger than life size, and represents Mr. Dawson in the act of addressing a public meeting. It is covered by a canopy, forty feet in height and supported by four granite columns; and it has four gables, each of which contains in medallion form a head, carved in bold relief, typical of religion, letters, statesmanship, and poetry. The portraits chosen are those of Bunyan, Carlyle, Cromwell, and Shakespeare. To the left of the Chamberlain memorial, is **a Statue of Sir Josiah Mason**, one of Birmingham's merchant princes, who amassed a large fortune by the manufacture of pens, and devoted a considerable portion of it to the establishment of—

### The Mason Science College,

a lofty pile of Thirteenth Century Gothic design, from designs by Mr. J. A. Cossins, which rears its noble proportions to the north of the square. With its hundred rooms and three hundred and seventy windows, the edifice rises to a height of a hundred and twenty-two feet, and occupies an area of more than two-thousand four hundred square yards. The object of the institution is to afford a thorough scientific education, especially with reference to manufactures, to mines and metallurgy, and to the laws of health. Sir Josiah Mason endowed the college with property consisting of freehold land and houses in Birmingham, yielding upwards of £3,000 a year, and paid all the expense of building and fittings —about £60,000. As he also founded and endowed an orphanage at Erdington, at the cost of more than a quarter of a million, an idea may be formed both of his wealth and of his beneficence. The college was opened in the autumn of 1880. It contains a **Bust of Dr. Heslop**, by Williamson. Adjoining the college, is—

### King Edward's High School for Girls,

originally intended as the home of the Birmingham Liberal Club. It was designed by Mr. J. A. Cossins; and proving too capacious for the club, it was temporarily devoted to its present purpose,* for which it is

* The governors are about to erect a commodious building for it, on the site of the "Hen and Chickens Restaurant," adjoining the Boys' High School in New Street.

very suitable. There are numerous class-rooms and every other requisite for the higher education of three hundred girls, some of whom attend the school till they attain the age of nineteen years.

The Mason Science College and the High School for Girls front *Edmund Street*, an important thoroughfare which runs eastward, parallel to and a little to the north of Colmore Row, as far as the Great Western Railway Station. About halfway along it, and fronting it and *Margaret Street* (which goes northward from it), is—

### The Municipal School of Art,

a handsome Gothic structure, opened in 1885. It stands on a plot of ground given for the purpose by Mr. Cregoe Colmore, and was built by subscriptions, Miss Ryland contributing £10,000, and Messrs. Richard and George Tangye, a similar sum, to the fund. The designs were almost completed by Mr. J. H. Chamberlain, at the time of his death; and were then entrusted by the committee to his partner, Mr. Martin, who successfully carried them out. The school is one of the most successful in the kingdom.

### The Medical Library and Institute,

the library originally a portion of the Birmingham Old Library but attached to the institute, on its foundation in 1878, are also in Edmund Street.

To the west of Chamberlain Square, we see—

### The Central Free Library,

a handsome edifice, alike worthy of the town and of the purpose to which it is devoted. It consists of two storeys, the lower one containing the news room and lending library, and the upper, the reference library (which is adorned by Williamson's **Bust of Mr. S. Timmins, F.S.A.**) The Free Libraries Act was adopted in the early part of 1860, and the Central Library was erected in 1865-6. It continued in existence till January 11, 1879, when it was entirely destroyed by fire. But here again the indomitable energy and public spirit which has made Birmingham what it is was displayed by its inhabitants. They immediately set to work to repair the loss, and entered into the matter with such vigour that the new library was opened in June, 1882; and help to replace the valuable literary treasures they had lost was given by "all sorts and conditions of" persons in the kingdom, from the Queen downwards. *The News Room is open daily from nine in the morning till ten at night; the Lending Library, from ten in the morning till nine at night; and the Reference Library, on week-days, from ten in the morning till ten at night, and on Sundays, from three till nine in the afternoon.*

The splendid building next to the Free Library, is the—

## Birmingham and Midland Institute.

It is a lofty edifice, of Italian architecture with a Corinthian colonnade, from designs by Sir E. M. Barry, the architect of the Houses of Parliament; its foundation stone was laid by the late Prince Consort, in 1855; and among its

STATUE OF WATT.

early presidents were Charles Dickens, Dean Stanley, Professors Huxley and Tyndall, &c. A wing, which contains a large and handsome lecture hall, a news room, class rooms, &c., was added in 1881. It is "a great educational institution of an essentially public character," and contains a museum, laboratory, lecture rooms, news and class rooms, &c. *The charge for admission varies from a shilling to twopence, at various periods of the year. An annual subscription of a guinea confers certain privileges: and one of two guineas, of course, carries with it an enlargement of them.*

As we reach the end of the street—

## The Statue of Watt,

considered the finest in the city arrests our attention. It stands between the Town Hall and the Midland Institute, on which spot it was placed in 1868, and is of Sicilian marble, by the late Alexander Munro. The inventor of the steam engine holds a pair of compasses in his right hand, and his left rests on the cylinder of an engine. It was thus described by the *Daily Post*, at the time when it was unveiled :—

"It would be difficult to conceive an attitude more thoroughly expressive of a work accomplished. The significant grasp of the engine by the left hand, and the almost dreamy way in which the other hand holds the compasses with their points upturned, tell the whole story of the man's life even to the careless spectator; for, useless as the compasses are now, and though still held, no longer active, the man rests secure in the knowledge of the greatness of his great invention. The statue is a poem, a great and noble work, which makes us glad when we think that we have such artists among us and of us; for the whole life is there, the innate genius, the long struggle, the many failures, the perfect victory and the triumph— one, indeed, unsoiled by any ignoble thought and into which entered no taint of earthly selfishness. The sculptor has seen the whole of Watt's life clearly, and he has made it plain to us also."

## The Queen's College,

on the opposite side of the street, is an imposing Tudor structure, built in 1843-4, and incorporated by Act of Parliament in 1867. The institution was founded, as the School of Medicine and Surgery by Mr. Sands Cox, in

1828. The *College Chapel*, constructed in 1844, contains a beautiful window of stained glass, and a silver altarpiece, by Sir E. Thomason, representing "The Shield of Faith." Three pictures by Jacques Louis David are hung in the dining hall.

\* \* \* \* \*

Leaving the Town Hall, and walking down *New Street* (in spite of its name one of the oldest in the city, but at the same time one of the finest), our attention is first claimed by the building occupied by—

### The Royal Birmingham Society of Artists,

which stands on the left-hand side. It is in the Corinthian style and constructed of Bath stone, its finely constructed portico projecting over the pavement. Completed in 1829, it includes a magnificent circular exhibition room and other apartments, where the annual exhibitions of modern artists are held. Its spring and autumn exhibitions of pictures are among the events of the year in Birmingham; and its Saturday afternoon concerts are noteworthy among the "functions" of the city.

A few steps further, on the opposite side, is—

### The Masonic Hall,

the foundation stone of which was laid by Lord Leigh, P.G.M., on Sept. 20, 1865. Upstairs, there is a large **Assembly Room**; and the **Midland Club** (non-political) has its home in the building. The following is a list of the Masonic Lodges, &c., in Birmingham, with the place and time of their ordinary meetings:—

*LODGES OF MASTER MASONS.*

*St. Paul's*, 43 [1733], Masonic Hall, New Street, fourth Monday from October to May, at 4.30 p.m.

*Athol*, 74 [1774], Masonic Hall, Severn Street, first Wednesday, at 6 p.m.

*Light*, 468 [1840], Great Western Hotel, third Tuesday from October to April.

*Faithful*, 473 [1841], Masonic Hall, New Street, second Tuesday.

*Howe*, 587 [1851], Masonic Hall, New Street, second Monday from October to May, at 4 p.m.

*Temperance*, 739 [1858], Masonic Hall, New Street, second Tuesday, except in July and August, at 5 p.m.

*Leigh Lodge of Rifle Volunteers*, 887 [1861], Masonic Hall, New Street, fourth Wednesday from October to May.
*Bedford*, 925 [1862], Masonic Hall, New Street, third Monday, at 5 p.m.
*Grosvenor*, 938 [1862], Masonic Hall, New Street, third Wednesday from September to April, at 5 p.m.
*Elkington*, 1016 [1864], Masonic Hall, New Street, fourth Tuesday, at 5 p.m.
*Fletcher*, 1031 [1864], Masonic Hall, New Street, second Wednesday, except July and August.
*Emulation*, 1163 [1867], Masonic Hall, New Street, fourth Thursday, at 5 p.m.
*Forward*, 1180 [1867], Masonic Hall, New Street, first Monday, except July, August, and September, at 5 p.m.
*Holte*, 1246 [1868], Victoria Hotel, Aston, third Wednesday, except June, July, and August.
*Israel*, 1474 [1874], Masonic Hall, Severn Street, second Monday in every month.
*Charity*, 1551 [1875], Masonic Hall, New Street, third Tuesday from September to May.
*Alma Mater*, 1644 [1876], Masonic Hall, New Street, third Friday in March, June, October, and January.

## ROYAL ARCH CHAPTERS.

*Fortitude*, 43 [1821], Great Western Hotel, second Tuesday in March, June, September, and December.
*Athol*, 74 [1862], Masonic Hall, Severn Street, fourth Tuesday in February, May, August, and November, at 6 p.m.
*Howe*, 587 [1855], Masonic Hall, New Street, first Thursday in February, May, August, and November, at 4 p.m.
*Grosvenor*, 938 [1864], Masonic Hall, New Street, first Tuesday in February, May, August, and November.
*Elkington*, 1016 [1870], Masonic Hall, New Street, first Thursday in January, April, July, and October.
*Fletcher*, 1031 [1867], Masonic Hall, New Street, first Tuesday in March, June, September, and December.

## MARK MASTER LODGES.

*Bedford*, 115 [1870], Masonic Hall, New Street, first Tuesday in January, April, July, and October, at 6 p.m.
*Athol*, 174 [1874], Masonic Hall, Severn Street, second Wednesday in March, June, September, and December, at 6 p.m.
*Howe*, [time immemorial], Great Western Hotel, second Tuesday in February, and third in May and September.
*Howe Preceptory of Knight Templars*, Masonic Hall, New Street, second Friday in February, and fourth in May and November, at 4 p.m.
*Vernon Chapter of S.P.R.C. of H.R.D.M.*, Great Western Hotel, first Friday in February, fourth in June, and third in October.

Continuing our eastward course, we next reach—

### The Theatre Royal,

the third which has stood on the site. Each of the two former was consumed by fire—the first, erected in 1774, in 1792, and the second, opened three years later, in 1820. The present building was erected in the same year, from the designs of the late Mr. Beasley. Its front is attractive; it consists of a piazza, surrounded by a colonnade, and ornamented with wings at the extremities, in the face of which are medallions, representing Shakespeare and Garrick.

Hutton gives an amusing history of "theatrical exhibitions in Birmingham," from which it appears that in 1730, the only theatre was "something like a stable in Castle Street." In 1740, three theatres are mentioned by Dr. Langford—one in New Street, a second in Smallbrook Street, and a third in Moor Street. The two former did not last long. The other was converted into a Wesleyan Chapel in 1764, a more commodious theatre having been erected in King Street, in 1752, and enlarged in 1774, the year in which the first was erected on the site of the Theatre Royal. The King Street Theatre competed with its rival with varying success for many years; but was ultimately converted into a chapel for the followers of Lady Huntingdon, to which purpose it was devoted till the removal of the chapel and street, some years since. The New Street Theatre was connected with the elder and younger Macready, and was constituted a theatre royal, by Act of Parliament, 1807. While on the subject, we may mention that there are three other theatres in Birmingham, one—the *Grand*—in Corporation Street—the second—the *Prince of Wales*—in Broad Street; and the third—the *Queen's*—on Snow Hill.

At No. 58, in this street, opposite the Colonnade Hotel, the imposing front whereof we notice on our right, is the Photographic Studio of Mr. Harold Baker, an artist who has carried off quite an array of silver and bronze medals in his competitions with his brethren of the camera in various parts of the kingdom. We are indebted for some of our illustrations to his sun-pictures; and he has obtained the post of photographer to the archæological section of the Birmingham and Midland Institute, an appointment which guarantees the excellence of his out-door work. Those of our friends who desire to "secure their shadows ere their substance perish"— to give correct presentments of their features to their relatives and neighbours—will find, on a visit to the studio, that Mr. Baker is not dependent on the smiles of Phœbus for the gratification of that desire; but that, availing himself of the modern discoveries of science, he has pressed the electric light into his service.

As we make our way along the street, we admire the architecture of the shops and other edifices. In the *Burlington Chambers*, we find another fine art society, rejoicing in the title of the **Art Circle**, whose exhibitions possess attractions specially their own, and whose membership includes many rising local artists. Adjoining it, is the **Midland Hotel**, a large edifice, the chief entrance to which faces the New Street railway station.

We next reach *Stephenson Place*, a wide opening, leading direct to the station. In the centre of the roadway, and on a line with New Street, is the **Statue of** "**Thomas Attwood**, founder of the Birmingham Political Union." (We quote its inscription.) The shaft, of gray granite, rests on a base of freestone, the statue itself being constructed of Sicilian marble. Erected in 1859, it was the work of the late Mr. John Thomas, of London, and represents Attwood in the act of addressing a public meeting. Its base is made gay with flowers.

Turning down Stephenson Place, we reach the gateway of—

## The New Street Railway Station,

the chief "depôt" of the London and North-Western and Midland Railway Companies in Birmingham. The front forms the **Queen's Hotel**, to which access is obtained direct from the platform. It is a handsome building in the Italian style, and consists of a centre and right and left wings. Considerable additions were made to the station in 1885. It now covers eleven acres of ground;

THE EXCHANGE.

and it is claimed for it that it is the largest railway station in the world. The centre is four storeys high, the lower storey being composed of an arcade, divided by Doric pilasters into ten arches, each pilaster is flanked by piers of rusticated masonry. The wings are only three storeys high. The platforms, of which there are thirteen—eight main and five side ones—are a quarter of a mile long; and the semicircular roof (of glass and corrugated iron), covering the older portion of the station, is eleven hundred feet long, two hundred and twelve feet wide, and eighty high. It is supported by forty-five massive Doric piers, springing from the station wall, on the one side, and by iron columns of a similar order, on the other. The bridge, which crosses the station is, by permission of the railway company (who occasionally accentuate their right to its user, by closing it against "strangers"), made use of as a public thoroughfare.

The eastern side of Stephenson Place, and a good slice of New Street, is occupied by—

## The Birmingham Exchange,

which was opened in 1865, to supply the long-felt want of a central meeting-place for men of business. It is a handsome pile of stone; its façade to Stephenson Place is a hundred and eighty feet long, and that to New Street about sixty-three. Its principal front, four storeys in height, is lighted by arched windows, and is ornamented by columns with richly carved capitals; and the building has a high-pitched roof, covered with parti-coloured slates. Over the central doorway, is a tower, terminating in a spire a hundred feet high; and there is a turret at the corner of the edifice. The ground floor is utilised as shops; and the Chamber of Commerce has its rooms in the building, whereof Mr. Edward Holmes was the architect.

Immediately opposite Stephenson Place is *Corporation Street*, one of the finest thoroughfares in Birmingham, along which we hope to make our way, by-and-bye.

## King Edward's Grammar School

(to give it the title by which it is legally known, the *Boys' High School, New Street*), closely adjacent to the Exchange, was founded in 1552, and endowed by Edward VI. with a portion of the property of the Guild of the Holy Cross, which had been "requisitioned" by his father. Though only valued at £21 at that time, the land thus granted now yields an enormous revenue, which is likely to increase with the lapse of years, for the property includes portions of the principal streets of the town. The school was at first held in the ancient hall of the guild, which was built in 1383; but that becoming worn out, it was in 1707 super-

KING EDWARD'S GRAMMAR SCHOOL.

seded by a larger building, ornamented by a tower, in which was a clock and bell, and, says Hutton, "a sleepy figure of the founder." This building in its turn fell into decay; and in 1832 it was removed and the present school erected in its place. It is a handsome Tudor-Gothic structure, one hundred and seventy-four by one hundred and twenty-five feet, and sixty in height; it was designed by Sir Edward Barry. It is quadrangular in form, the entrance being through a spacious porch, highly ornamented. There are two large rooms, one for the classical and the other for the commercial school. The building, too, contains a good library and a boardroom, in which is a fine bust of Edward VI., by Scheemaker. In connection with the Grammar School, there are twelve exhibitions at the Oxford and Cambridge universities. Besides this school, the estate supports the *Girls' High School*, in Colmore Row and branch schools at Five Ways at Aston, Bath Row, Camp Hill, and Summer Hill.

And now, passing the *Hen and Chickens Restaurant*,* in its time a famous coaching house, the portico of which extends over the pavement, we reach the end of New Street and glance down Worcester Street, on our right; and then we make our way into the Bull Ring, in the centre of which is—

### St. Martin's Church

[Services on Sundays, at 10.45, 3.30, and 6.30; Hymnal Companion],

the mother church of Birmingham. The date of the consecration of the original edifice is unknown; it is not mentioned in Domesday Book, but we find that, in 1330, Walter de Clodsdale founded a chantry "at the altar of the blessed Virgin Mary in the Church of St. Martin at Birmingham." Hutton, who always claimed a high antiquity for his adopted town, infers—though he does not assert—that the edifice was in existence before the Norman Conquest. In 1690, the churchwardens (to adopt the words of Bunce) "dressed the church in brick—tower, nave, and chancel;" so that "the whole fabric was there buried in an ugly tomb—literally bricked up, as if, like unhappy Constance in 'Marmion,' it had committed an unexpiable sin and had received the sentence of living death." Referring to this "restoration," Hutton says that "the rough blasts of *nine hundred years* had made inroads on the fabric." We do not know on what ground

* The restaurant is soon to be pulled down to make room for the Girls' High School.

ST. MARTIN'S CHURCH.

he bases his calculation, and must leave the nut for antiquaries to crack. The church was restored in 1733 and 1781 ; but it continued to wear its brick case till 1872, when the edifice was pulled down and rebuilt in the Early Decorated style from designs by Mr. Chatwin, of Birmingham. It was consecrated on July 10, 1875. it is a hundred and fifty-three feet long by sixty-seven wide ; and is a noble and beautiful church, which the inhabitants "show with pride to strangers, and with all the greater pride because from first to last—design, building, fittings, and enrichments, it is a Birmingham work." The tower and spire had been previously rebuilt in 1853-5, and these form part of the new church ; the spire is a hundred and twenty-seven feet and a half high. The church is enriched with memorial and other painted windows, and contains four of the altar tombs of the early lords of Birmingham. Lofty arches, preserved from the old church, connect the north aisle with the tower ; and the chancel arch rises to the full height of the roof of the nave. The latter has a beautiful clerestory, and an open-timbered roof, not unlike that of Westminster Abbey.

Immediately in front of the church is a—

### Statue of Nelson,

It is of bronze, and was the work of Westmacott, and, as the inscription on its base informs us, " was erected by the inhabitants of Birmingham, A.D. MDCCCIX." The figure is clothed in uniform ; his left arm resting on an anchor, with a model of a man-o'-war behind him. It stands on a marble pedestal ; and is, to quote the artist's own words, " enclosed by iron palisades, in the form of boarding pikes, connected by a twisted cable ; and at each of the four corners is fixed a cannon erect, from which issues a lamp post, representing a cluster of pikes, supporting a ship lantern." Mr. Joseph Farror, a local auctioneer, bequeathed sixpence per week for ever, to be expended in keeping clean the statue and its basement ; though whether this munificent bequest will entirely account for its present good condition, " this deponent sayeth not."

The *Bull Ring* is the market-place of Birmingham. At the point where High Street joins it, we see—

## The Market Hall,

extending back to Worcester Street, to which it has a front; its sides occupy the entire length of Bell and Phillip Streets. It is a fine building of Bath stone, dating from 1833, and was designed by Mr. Charles Edge; it is three hundred and sixty-five feet long, a hundred and eight feet wide, and sixty high, and it has a covered area of 39,411 square feet. Before its erection, the old fashion of holding the market in the open air prevailed in Birmingham.

The **Fish Market** is at the opposite corner of Bell Street; the **Meat** or **Carcase Market** is in Bradford Street, not far off; and at a short distance south of the church is **Smithfield Market**, occupying the site of the castle of the lords of Birmingham, of which we speak on p. 5. While on the subject, we may mention—

## The Corn Exchange,

the chief entrance to which is from High Street, but which has a door from Carr's Lane, a thoroughfare connecting that street with Moor Street. The Corn Exchange was opened in 1847. Its interior, of Italian Doric architecture, is pleasing. The vaulted room, a hundred and seventy-two feet long and from thirty-seven to forty wide, is divided into three compartments by rows of pillars. Adjoining it, are the old magistrates' courts—"disestablished," when the Victoria Law Courts were opened, and destined, so sayeth "many tongued-rumour," some day to be a railway terminus.

### St. Michael's Roman Catholic Chapel

[Sunday services at 8.0, 9.30, 11.0, 4.0, and 6.30],

in Moor Street, is an historic edifice—the celebrated New Meeting, which took the place of the edifice burnt during the "Church and King" riots. When the congregation built the Church of Messiah (which *see*), they sold this edifice to the Roman Catholics, who consecrated it and dedicated it to St. Michael.

### Carr's Lane Congregational Chapel

[Sunday services at 10.45 and 6.30],

the chief place of worship belonging to that body in Birmingham, occupies the site of the first Independent chapel in the place. It has been twice rebuilt, the last time in 1819, when the foundation stone was laid by the celebrated John Angell James, its then minister, an office which he held for upwards of fifty years; and it has since then been twice repaired and enlarged—in 1844 and 1876.

If, before leaving the neighbourhood, we continued our walk from the Bull Ring in a south-easterly direction, we should, after passing through Digbeth, cross the river Rea, and reach Leland's "propper chappell," or rather its successor—

### The Church of St. John the Baptist.

[Sunday services at 11.0 and 6.30; Hymnal Companion.]

The present brick church was erected in 1735, on the site of one of the earliest results of the teaching of John Wycliffe. It is an Italian edifice, with a square pinnacled tower, dating from 1702; and the peal of "eight most musical bells, together with a clock, entered the steeple," says Hutton. On the south side of the chancel, is a marble bust of John Rogers, a native of Deritend, the first martyr burnt at Smithfield in the reign of Mary the Bloody; the bust was from the studio of Mr. E. G. Papworth, of London, and was unveiled in 1883.

In the neighbourhood of the church is the "mansion house of tymber" at "Dirtey"—the Old Crown House already referred to, in one room of which "good Queen Bess" is said to have slept.

But our course lies not that way to-day; and we must hasten on. Leaving the Bull Ring, we walk, northward, along *High Street* to its junction with Dale End, Albert Street, and Bull Street, where we reach another of those "salient angles which afford scope for fine buildings," of which the site of the Town Hall, &c., is one. But here we find no public building, though we are at no great distance from—

## St. Peter's Church.

[Services as follows: Holy Communion on the first and third Sundays of the month, at 8.0 a.m.; on the second, third, fourth, and fifth, at 11.15. Morning service, on the first Sunday, at 11.0; on the second, third, fourth, and fifth at 10.40. Evening service at 6.30. Hymns Ancient and Modern.]

This edifice, of Anglo-Grecian architecture, was built, from plans by Rickman and Hutchinson (architects who have left their mark on Birmingham), in 1825-7, when "the expense of the site and structure," so the inscription on a brass plate, embedded in mortar under the foundation stone, informs us, "amounting to £19,676 2s. 11d., was defrayed out of a parliament grant of £1,000,000," voted for church-building in the town. The west end—that facing the street—is ornamented by a tetrastyle Doric portico, surmounted by an octagonal turret, at the corners whereof are Doric pillars. The portico was copied from that of the Temple of Minerva at Athens, and in its construction some massive stones, from Guiting, in Gloucestershire, were used. Four years after its erection, the interior of the church was gutted by fire; and its restoration occupied six years.

From the end of High Street, lines of street diverge to all the north-eastern suburbs, and particularly to *Aston Park*, which we intend visiting on another occasion. Enjoying our "window parade" along *Bull Street*, our attention is occupied by its shops of attractive architecture, whose windows glitter with all kinds of merchandise. We cross *Corporation Street*, and soon afterwards we reach (on our right) the entrance to the principal—

## Meeting House of the Society of Friends.

[Sunday services at 10.30 and 6.30.]

The earliest record of the presence of the Friends in Birmingham is in 1655. Their original "meeting" was in Monmouth Street, but they removed to their present home between 1702 and 1705. The meeting-house, described by Hutton as "a large and convenient place, and, notwithstanding the plainness of their profession, rather elegant," after being very much altered and twice enlarged, was removed, and the present edifice erected in its place. It was designed by Mr. T. Plevins, and opened in January, 1857.

A few steps further, and, at the head of the street, we reach the *Great Western Hotel*, adjoining and connected with—

## The Great Western Railway Station,

on Snow Hill, a two-storeyed structure, to which red brick string courses and moulded corbels and cornices of Bath stone impart an ornamental character. It has two fronts; the one on the Livery Street side being similar to that facing Snow Hill, but consisting of only one storey. The roof over the main line is of wrought iron and glass, similar to that at the New Street station; but it is much smaller. It is five hundred feet long and ninety-one in span. The platforms are spacious, and the station contains waiting and refreshment rooms and every other adjunct necessary for the comfort of the numerous passengers by the numerous trains which pass through the station.

But the hotel, which faces Colmore Row, and partly surmounts the tunnel by means of which the line burrows its way through the heart of the town, has a more attractive appearance than the station. It is a handsome Italian edifice of white brick, with Bath stone dressings.

At the head of Bull Street, several large and well-frequented arteries strike off in various directions. Here are *Snow Hill* and *Steelhouse Lane*, which afford means of access to important outlying districts, as a reference to our map will show. But we shall visit these two arteries on another occasion; and to-day direct our steps along *Colmore Row*, the northern side of the triangle through which we have been (in imagination) making our way. And a noble vista it presents, as we stand opposite the Great Western Hotel and look westward. Wide and spacious, its northern side is of quite recent construction. Its *tout ensemble* conveys to the eyes a pleasing impression of the enterprise of the sons of Birmingham, and is a satisfactory outward and visible sign of their prosperity. Besides the Great Western—

## The Grand Hotel

greets the eye, a few yards further on. It presents a façade to the street which cannot fail to attract the most superficial observer and to convince him that the name is happily chosen; and a more intimate acquaintance with it and its comforts increases the good opinion which the stranger had

THE GRAND HOTEL.

formed of it. It is lighted throughout by electricity; its floors are reached by passenger elevators; and every modern convenience is placed at the disposal of its guests. Immediately on entering the spacious hall, one is struck with the comfort of the appointments of the hotel. All the public rooms, as well as the private suites of apartments, are luxuriously furnished; and its two hundred bedrooms are cosy and comfortable. The billiard-room in the basement fitted with four of Thurston's best tables is pronounced to be the finest in the country; and there is a hairdressing saloon for the convenience of ladies and gentlemen in the hotel. The principal feature of the recent extensive additions is a magnificent suite of rooms, for banquets, balls, &c., which will supply a long-felt want in the Midlands.

Among the public edifices which ornament the line of buildings, is—

## The Union Club

(non-political)—the first club established in Birmingham. The club-house is a splendid stone edifice of Italian architecture, which will bear comparison with the palaces which ornament Club-land in the West End of London. Its exterior is decorated by columns of the Corinthian order, and the fittings of the interior are in keeping with its outward appearance.

The railings of St. Philip's Churchyard occupy the chief portion of the south side of the street; and the perspective is appropriately closed by the Council House and the magnificent group of buildings standing on the spot where we commenced our walk.

## St. Philip's Church.

[The services on Sundays commence at 10.45, 3.30, and 6.30; children are publicly catechised during the afternoon service on the first and third Sundays of the month. Hymns Ancient and Modern.]

St. Philip's, the second parish church in Birmingham, was begun in 1711, consecrated in 1715, and finished in 1719. Its site is said to be eighty feet higher than the top of the cross of St. Paul's, London, and the church was built in imitation of the metropolitan cathedral, from designs by Thomas Archer, a pupil of Wren. It is composed of stone; is a hundred and forty feet long by seventy-five wide; and is capable of holding eighteen hundred persons. In the tower, are chimes and a peal of ten bells. The nave was thoroughly restored in 1864, and the chancel was lengthened in 1884. The exterior is ornamented by a row of Doric pilasters (between which are the windows), supporting a handsome balustrade. Hutton ascribes its dedication to St. Philip to a desire

ST. PHILIP'S CHURCH.

to honour the donor of the site, a Mr. Phillips—" in

THE BLUE COAT SCHOOL.

order," he says, "to perpetuate his memory and enable him to share with the saintly patron a red-letter day in the calendar." He describes the church as a "superb edifice," and adds :—

"When I first saw St. Philip's, in the year 1741, at a proper distance, uncrowded with houses—for there were none to the north, New Hall excepted—untarnished with smoke, and illuminated by a western sun, I was delighted with its appearance, and thought it then, what I do now, and what others will in future, the pride of the place."

Our engraving will enable our readers to form an accurate opinion of the justice of Hutton's verdict; we are sure they will endorse it. The office of rector of the parish is now held by the bishop suffragan of Coventry, and in that way the salary of that official is assured.

The **Churchyard** contains the graves and epitaphs of many generations of the inhabitants of the parish, as well as memorials of some who are not buried there, and of others not directly connected with the city. The most prominent of them all is the **Monument to Colonel Burnaby**, near the southern railings. It was erected by the subscriptions of persons of all shades of political thought, a considerable sum being contributed by the working men of the city; and it was unveiled in November, 1885, by Lord Charles Beresford. The edifice consists of a basement of three massive steps of Hopton woodstone, a moulded pedestal, and an obelisk of Portland stone; and it is altogether fifty feet high. In a niche on the south side, is a marble bust of the colonel. On the other side, are cut the words, "Burnaby—Khiva, 1870; Abou Klea, 1885." Over the bust, is a trophy, consisting of the helmet and cuirass of his regiment (the Blues), spears, guns, &c., and the primrose ornaments the upper moulding of the pedestal.

\*　　\*　　\*　　\*　　\*

It is not our intention to proceed straight to our journey's end; we shall make a *détour* on our way. But before doing so, we must not overlook—

## The Blue Coat School,

located in an extensive building facing Colmore Row and

the eastern side of St. Philip's churchyard. It is one of those charitable and beneficent institutions which are the pride and glory of the city and indeed of the country at large. It is entirely supported by voluntary contributions, but by careful and judicious management it maintains and educates two hundred orphan boys and girls, whom it fits for the active duties of life. The school itself was originated in 1724, the handsome stone front which faces the street being added in 1794, when nearly £3,000 was expended in improving the building. Over the principal entrance are figures of a boy and girl, habited in the quaint costume of the school; but these form the only attempt at ornamentation (and they were paid for by an independent subscription), those having the control of the matter wisely preferring to expend the funds at their control in erecting a substantial fabric and promoting the well-being of the school.

We have been standing, while discoursing of the features of the handsome thoroughfare before us, at the terminus of the cable tramway, whose comfortable vehicles (every five minutes during the day) start on their journeys to many of the northern suburbs of the city—Handsworth and Hockley, amongst them. We are close to the northern end of—

### The Great Western and North-Western Arcades,

an imposing connecting link between Colmore Row and Corporation Street. Their glass roof is forty feet in height, the centre being ornamented by a beautifully designed dome. Together, they form a promenade, a favourite resort of ladies, when "shopping." The first-named arcade extends as far as Temple Row, a distance of some four hundred yards, and was erected in 1876. The North-Western Arcade was added about half a dozen years later. Walking along the covered way, and admiring the artistic goods in the windows of the shops by which we are surrounded, we reach Temple Row, nearly opposite—

THE GREAT WESTERN ARCADE.

## Ye Olde Royal Hotel,

an edifice of historic interest. It was built by subscription, on the tontine system, and completed in 1772; and in Hutton's time it was *the* hotel of the town, for there was no other establishment worthy of the name. The historian tells us that "the pile itself is large, plain, and elegant," with "a handsome entrance." In his day, assemblies were held there weekly, and he says, the apartments of the hotel "give room for beauty to figure at cards, at conversation, and in the dance." Many Masonic gatherings took place in it; and here was held the dinner, in celebration of the anniversary of the first French Revolution, which was made the pretext for the "Church and King" riots of 1791. Here, too, the Duke of Wellington and Sir Robert Peel were entertained at dinner by the high bailiff (the predecessor of the mayor of the present day) in 1830; and here the Princess Victoria took up her quarters, when visiting the town in the same year. Mr. Dent, in his "Old and New Birmingham," mentions a somewhat unusual display of loyalty on that occasion by a Mrs. Fairfax, who lived in Great Charles Street. He says :—

"A guard of honour waited in St. Philip's Churchyard, so as to be near the hotel, commanded by the Hon. Grantham M. Yorke, who afterwards became rector of the noble church hard by and is now [1879] dean of Worcester. As the time drew near for the arrival of the royal visitors, the military escort was drawn up in front of the hotel, chiefly for the purpose of doing the work which should have been done by the police, had there been any in that day. Discipline was but indifferently preserved in the large crowd which had assembled; and as the future queen of England alighted from the carriage, a lady suddenly rushed forward from the front ranks of the crowd and, snatching the astonished little royal lady into her arms, fervently kissed her. The crowd cheered loudly at this exhibition of exuberant loyalty and impulsive affection; but the royal party showed considerable annoyance and even anger."

A writer in 1826 declared that the hotel was the central point of the borough. It was later on used as the temporary home of the Birmingham Eye Hospital; and it now takes a foremost rank among the restaurants of the city, its admirable cuisine and appointments reminding many of the numerous excellent banquets that have been enjoyed within its portals.

## The Conservative Club House,

opened in 1887, is a spacious edifice of Italian architecture, designed by Messrs. Osborn and Reading, and presenting to the street a well-proportioned portico and boldly projecting balconies.

Walking along *Temple Row*, we reach the corner of *Temple Street*, where is the *Central Temperance Hotel;* and then walking along Waterloo Street, we soon regain the **Peel Statue**, whence we started, and end our walk through the Centre of Birmingham.

---

## NEW STREET TO ASTON AND BACK.

STARTING on this excursion, we shall meet at the Attwood Statue and then cross *New Street*, and walk along *Corporation Street*, constructed by the municipal council between 1876 and 1880, at a cost of about a million and a half. It is a splendid wide street, cut straight through the most closely-built portion of the city, lined with fine edifices, and altogether worthy of its position in the centre of the chief city in the Midlands of England.

Near its commencement, it cuts through the junction of two important streets—*Cherry Street*, on the left, and *Union Street*, on the right. The former preserves the memory of a cherry orchard, which once flourished on the spot; it communicates with Temple Row along which we walked at the close of our last excursion. Union Street connects Corporation and High Streets; in it is—

### The Old Birmingham Library,

founded in 1779. It contains, in addition to a well-selected library, a news room, a ladies' drawing room, a gentlemen's reading and smoking room, &c. The building is of Classic design (by Mr. William Hollins), and was erected in 1797. It has two storeys, the lower one ornamented by coupled Roman Doric, and the upper one by Ionic pilasters. Its semi-circular portico bears a Latin inscription, from the pen of Dr. Samuel Parr. It was altered and extended in 1888. *Subscription, one guinea per annum.* In this street, too, is—

### The General Dispensary,

founded in 1794, and therefore the oldest of the medical charities in the city. It was at first "housed" in Temple Street; but in 1808, its premises becoming too small, the present building was erected from designs by Mr. W. Hollins. It consists of a centre and two wings, the former ornamented by a triangular pediment, supported by four pillars, with fluted capitals. A sculpture, over the door, represents a female with a cup of medicine in her hand, and bears the inscription, "Of the Most High, comes healing."

As we walk up Corporation Street, we have, on our right and left, large and imposing places of business, luxurious restaurants, and two of the best "houses of entertainment" in the city.

### The Cobden Temperance Hotel,

at the corner of Cherry Street, was opened with considerable *éclat* in 1888, its architectural features being such that it almost ranks among the public buildings of the city; and—

### The Victoria Hotel,

is equally attractive in its appearance. Internally, too, it possesses everything necessary to secure the comfort of its patrons. Its coffee and commercial rooms and its ladies' drawing room are comfortably — nay, even luxuriously — furnished. Its seventy bedrooms are airy and possessed of everything that could be desired to secure that great desideratum—a good night's rest. It is, moreover, lighted by electricity; its guests possess the advantage of telephonic communication (its number is 1,034); and while its position is central for business purposes, it is easily reached by the jaded traveller, for it is only about a hundred and eighty yards from the New Street station of the London and North-Western and Midland Railways and four hundred from that of the Great Western line at Snow Hill.

We pass the entrance to the *North-Western Arcade* and cross **Bull Street** (both of which we visited in our first walk). The **Stork Hotel,** the **Wesleyan Central Chapel,** and the adjoining **Central Hall** next present themselves, on the right; and then a few yards further, we reach the erstwhile *Old Square*, which the new boulevard has bisected diagonally. Here is the terminus of the line of tramcars to Aston, which we shall utilise by-and-bye, when we have seen what Corporation Street has to show us. On the south-eastern side of the street we notice—

## The Grand Theatre,

built (1883), in the French Renaissance style from the plans by Mr. Ward. Its auditorium is specially well designed, its shape and the convenience of its seats adding not a little to the comfort of the spectators. The size of the theatre fully justifies the "pet name" by which it is often spoken of, "the Drury Lane of the Midlands."

Walking onward for a few yards, we see, on the right, a block of chambers of charming elevation—presumably, tenanted by "limbs of the law," for it rejoices in the title of *Lincoln's Inn*. Nearly opposite, at the corner of *Newton Street*, is—

## The County Court,

constructed of Hollington stone and of Italian design (by Mr. James Williams); and almost adjoining it, are—

## The Victoria Law Courts,

as they are called, because, as witness the inscription on

the foundation stone, it " was laid by her Majesty Queen Victoria, on the 23rd March, in the year 1887, being the jubilee year of her reign." It was opened by the Prince and Princess of Wales four years later. The building, designed by Messrs. Webb and Bell, com-

THE VICTORIA LAW COURTS.

prises two large assize courts, three police courts, a coroner's court, the necessary retiring rooms, and so forth. A noteworthy feature in the building, both externally and internally, is the great hall, from which four of the courts open directly; it is a very fine apartment, eighty feet by forty. Its windows are filled with painted glass—a Jubilee memorial of the city of Birmingham.

The façade of the building is very richly treated in a free Renaissance, and is constructed entirely of red terra-cotta. The sculpture in the centre gable bears the royal arms, and in the flanking gables are emblematic figures by Mr. Aumonier, representing the arts and crafts in the trades of Birmingham. The richest portion is the central entrance porch, adorned by a statue of her Majesty, by Mr. Harry Bates, and four spandril figures representing the attributes of Justice, designed by Mr. Walter Crane and executed by Mr. Frith. Below the Queen, is a group of St. George and the Dragon. The whole building is crowned by a figure of Justice, by Mr. Frith, who also designed and executed the charming little figures on the summits of the turrets. Red terra-cotta was selected as being the best material for withstanding the atmosphere of Birmingham. Internally, the great hall, the court wall above the panelling, and the corridors are faced with buff terra-cotta; and the fittings and wall linings throughout are of oak. *The curator will show strangers over the building at any hour when it is open.* He will not refuse a "testimonial."

Nearly opposite the Law Courts, is **the Citadel of the Salvation Army**; and then we soon reach the end of Corporation Street; and climb to the top of a tramcar to ride to Aston. Our route lies along *Aston Street* and *Aston Road*. Scarcely have we started, when looking down *Gem Street*, on our right, we see some public schools and—

### Bishop Ryder's Church

[Sunday services at 11.0, 3.0, and 6.30; Hymns Ancient and Modern],

a Perpendicular structure of brick, with stone dressings. It has a lofty tower, copied on a small scale from that of St. Botolph, of Boston; and it was built in 1831-3, in memory of Bishop Ryder, of Lichfield.

Gosta Green, through which we drive, and which marks the boundary between Aston Street and Aston Road, is said to have obtained its name from its exposed position (advocates of this theory say that it is a corruption of the word "gusty"), or from the gorse in the neighbourhood ("gosty land" is still, in some parts of Warwickshire and Worcestershire, applied to land on which gorse grows). Hutton, however, traces the word to "goose strait," and says it was originally given to a "track of commons, circumscribed by the Stafford Road," just as goose green is often applied to the common on which the villagers in olden time had the right to turn their geese, &c. As we cross the green, we see, on our left, a branch of the *Free Library*. Next, we cross successively the **Birmingham and Fazeley Canal**, and the **Aston**, or **Hockley, Brook**, the latter the boundary between the parish of Birmingham and that of—

## Aston

(the name whereof may be literally translated "the east town"), which was, in the old times, a much more important place than Birmingham. Now, it forms a suburb of the city, to whose corporation belongs the hall where the lords of the manor resided when the rude forefathers of the town—the smiths of whom Leland and Camden tell us—were struggling onward and upward. The parish, which includes Bordesley, Deritend, Duddesley, and other portions of northern and eastern Birmingham, belonged in Saxon times to the earls of Mercia, and was bestowed by the Conqueror on Fitz-Ausculf, to whom Birmingham was also given. In Domesday book, it is valued at £5, five times as much as the latter place. The tables are turned to some purpose now. We need not enter into a history of the township, nor attempt to narrate the changes by which the manor eventually became the property of the Sir Thomas Holte, who built the hall, and of whom we shall have something to note by-and-by. Neither need we say anything of Aston in Saxon times. It is enough now to remind one another that four wards of the parish are now included in the city of Birmingham; that the rest—which has a population of nearly eighty thousand—is governed by a Local Board, with all the blessings that follow in its train; and that Aston has a School Board, fully alive to the responsibility of its position, and a Free Public Library.

At the junction of the *Avenue Road*, with that along which we are travelling (on our right), there stands—

### The Church of St. Mary's, Aston Brook

[Sunday services, 8.0, 10.45, 3.0, and 6.30; Hymns Ancient and Modern],

a modern Decorated building, consecrated in 1863, and conspicuous by its well-proportioned tower, rising to an altitude of a hundred and ten feet. Its chancel contains "storied" windows, commemorative of members of the family of the founder of the church, Mr. Josiah Robins.

We drive through what was, of old, the village street, now lined with good shops and so forth. As we proceed, we notice the **Theatre**, opened in 1893; and we soon reach the Gothic **Cross**, rebuilt in 1893, which marks the end of Aston Road and from which *Park Road* and *Lichfield Road, Tower Road, Park Lane,* and *Rocky Lane* diverge in opposite directions. We alight at the Cross, and make our way along *Park Road*, passing a **Congregational Church** (Sunday services at 11.0 and 6.30), on our right, just before we cross *Victoria Road;* and so we reach the gate of the graveyard, surrounding—

### Aston Parish Church

[Sunday services at 11.0, 3.0, and 6.30; Hymnal Companion],

dedicated to St. Peter and St. Paul. The date of the erection of this interesting structure has not been clearly ascertained. Its architecture is of the various styles in vogue in England from the thirteenth to the fifteenth century; and there is a record of the great tithes having been given to the Tickford Priory, at Newport Pagnell, Bucks, in the reign of Henry II., and of the grant being

ASTON PARISH CHURCH.

confirmed in 1231. It is surmised that the nave and a portion of the chancel were built at that time, and that the church gradually assumed its present shape during the years which its architecture would seem to indicate. It is known that the chancel was lengthened and otherwise altered in the reign of Edward II., and that the tower and spire were added in that of Henry VI., so that there is some probability of these guesses being nearer the truth than is sometimes the case. The edifice had, in the course of years, been "churchwardened" and otherwise disfigured, and time had left the impress of his fingers upon it. The services of Pugin were therefore secured by the parishioners some time ago; and later on the skill of Chatwin (the architect who rebuilt St. Martin's, Birmingham) was had recourse to. The latter so extensively restored the church as to almost rebuild it; and now all traces of the barbarous usage to which it was subjected have been removed and the fabric has been restored to its original beauty. Mr. Chatwin succeeded in renovating the spire and slightly added to its height.

The chancel contains four altar tombs in good preservation—one of them, that of Walter de Arden, bearing the date 1407; and in the north aisle of the nave the builder of Aston Hall sleeps beneath a similar monument, with this inscription upon the brass,

"Thomas Holte here lyeth in grave: Jhu for Thyn passyon,
On him Thou have compassyon: and his soolle do save."

Around the tomb runs a legend, enumerating his virtues and charitable deeds. In the chancel, are four stalls, interesting from the fact that they were brought from St. Margaret's at Leicester. They were removed from the chancel of that church and condemned as "rubbish"; and form only a small portion of the beautiful series, erected by Abbot Penny, who died in 1509, and which were greatly admired for their beauty. Some fine old antique stone seats were lately discovered within the altar rails; and a relic of the churchyard cross, of Early English date, is preserved in the chancel. It is ornamented by a representation of the Crucifixion and the Virgin and Child, and by figures of St. Peter and St. Paul. These, and some beautiful windows, restored by Pugin, are among the features most worth notice in this grand old church.

Almost opposite the church, is the chief entrance to—

## Aston Park and Hall,

purchased by the corporation of Birmingham in 1864, when the people of that town obtained in a peaceable manner a permanent possession of the building their predecessors took by force in Cromwell's days and then held for only a short period. The fact is thus recorded on a brass tablet in the entrance hall:—

> "Be it remembered that on the twenty-second day of September, A.D. 1864, and in the mayorality of the Rt. Worshipful William Holliday, Esq., this hall and forty-three acres of land surrounding it, having been purchased by the corporation of the borough of Birmingham, were formally dedicated to the use of the people for their recreation, as a free hall and park for ever. And be it also remembered that of the sum of twenty-six thousand pounds paid by the corporation, as the purchase money, the sum of £7,000 was contributed by the benevolent lady and gentlemen whose names and donations are inscribed below." [The lady referred to is Miss Louisa Anne Ryland, whose subscription was £1,000; other donations range from £2,000 to £100.]

The **Park**, which comprises forty-three acres, is only a part of the original one, some portion having fallen a prey to the demon of bricks and mortar before its purchase by the corporation. It is kept in beautiful order. The chief entrance is that known as the **Church Lodge**, close to which the tramcars stop. It has a large gate, spanned by a stone ogee arch, which is enriched by crockets and a finial, and two posterns, and is flanked by two cottages, decorated by the squirrel (the crest of the Holtes) and lighted by mullioned windows. Thence a carriage drive conducts us to the main avenue of chestnut trees and elms, of old nearly a mile in length, by which we reach—

The **Hall**, which is a noble edifice of Elizabethan architecture. To quote an inscription over its door—

> "Sir Thomas Holte, of Duddeston, in the Countie of Warwick, Knight and Baronet, began to build this House in Aprill in Anno Domini, 1618: in the sixteenth yeare of the reigne of King James of England, &c., and of Scotland the one and fiftieth; and the said Sir Thomas Holte came to dwell in this House in May, in Anno Domini, 1631, in the seventh yeare of the reigne of our Sovereigne Lord King Charles; and he did finish this House in Aprill, Anno Domini, 1635; in the eleventh yeare of the reigne of the said King Charles. *Laus Deo.*"

Within seven years of the completion of the Hall, the struggle between Charles and his Parliament commenced; and Sir Thomas Holte, a zealous Royalist, entertained the king for two nights previously to the battle of Edge Hill, an honour for which he afterwards paid dearly. Fearing an attack from the Parliamentarian forces in Birmingham, he applied to the governor of Dudley Castle for protection. Though he only obtained forty musketeers, he resisted the Roundheads, twelve hundred in number, for three days, and only capitulated when the Hall had suffered much from the artillery of the attacking party. The marks made by the balls are still pointed out. Sir Thomas was imprisoned for his loyalty, and so heavily fined, that, on his death, he left his estates sadly crippled. In 1782, the last of the Holtes having cut off the entail, the property passed out of the hands of the family, who had held it for four hundred and nineteen years. Hutton devotes several pages of his "History" to some quaint criticism of the occurrence, and concludes by saying:—

> "This ancient and worthy family, that sprang from the anvil, sported upon an estate worth £12,000 a year, but is now sunk into its pristine obscurity, for its head, Thomas Holte (perhaps Sir Thomas), at this day thumps at the anvil for bread in the fabrication of spades. A most amiable man as any of his race, and the only baronet that ever shaped a shovel, may take a melancholy ramble for miles upon the land of his ancestors, but cannot call one foot his own."

The estates passed into the possession of the Legge family, and were, in the year 1818, sold piecemeal, part of the land being bought by a member of Hutton's family. In 1830, James Watt, the son of the celebrated engineer, was living at the hall, where he was visited by the Princess Victoria, at that time staying at the Royal Hotel (*see* pp. 46-7). (Her Majesty has a reference to the visit in her "Diary.") Mr. Watt died in 1847; and in

ASTON PARK: THE CHURCH LODGE.

1856 (the park having been cut up and a portion built upon), the corporation, "desirous," we are told, "of preserving the historic hall, and of obtaining so desirable a park for the people," entered into negotiations for the purchase of what remained. They, however, failed in their endeavours; but the estate was bought by a limited liability company, and opened as a public—but not free —park by the Queen in June, 1858. In 1863, a fatal

ASTON HALL.

accident happened to a female rope-dancer, known as "The Female Blondin," at a Foresters' fête; and a letter was addressed to the Mayor (Mr. C. Sturge), by the Queen's direction, in which he was asked to use his "influence to prevent in future the degradation to such exhibitions of the park, which was gladly opened by her Majesty and the beloved Prince Consort, in the hope that it would be made serviceable for the healthy exercise and rational recreation of the people." The authorities renewed their endeavours for the purchase of the property; and, mainly owing to the exertions of Mr. George Dawson, were successful this time. The company were very liberal in their terms; and the corporation bought the park and hall in 1864, and threw it open to the public free of any charge.

The Hall occupies the summit of a gentle eminence, its time-worn front impressing the beholder with its stateliness. Its plan consists of a main building, with two wings extending forward, after the manner of Elizabethan edifices (this was built in the early years of James I.); and its chief features are large windows (the front one in the wings embayed) and three lofty towers, surmounted by ogee-shaped roofs. The central tower is of three storeys, and contains a clock. The Hall is now used as a museum. The stables have been converted into refreshment rooms—very welcome on a hot summer day.

## Aston Lower Grounds,

adjoining the park, are in the hands of a company. They are now used as the rendezvous of the athletes of Birmingham and North Warwickshire; and they contain a large hall, two hundred and twenty feet long by ninety wide, &c., in which Sunday concerts and other gatherings are held.

We may, if we are pressed for time, return to Corporation Street by tramcar; but those desirous of seeing a little more of Aston before doing so, will follow *Trinity*

*Road*, for a few yards, after leaving Aston Park by its north-western gates. Turning to the left, along *Witton Road*, we pass, at the spot where *Albert Road* (which communicates with Park Road) crosses that by which we are progressing—

## The Aston Public Offices and Free Library.

They occupy a red brick edifice, designed, in the Queen Anne style, by Mr. W. Henman, the erection whereof cost £10,000.

A little to the west of their front, we pass **Christ Church** (*Baptist*) [*Sunday services at* 11.0 *and* 6.30]; and a few doors to its westward reach an open space, rejoicing in the title of *Six Ways*, so named because it forms the junction of six main streets. They are, Witton Road, Victoria Road, Birchfield Road, High Street, Lozells Road, and Alma Street.

A walk along the *Lozells Road* will enable us to visit the **Lozells Congregational Church** [*Sunday services at* 11.0 *and* 6.30], which, facing *Wheeler Street*, and built in 1839, is described as one of the largest Nonconformist places of worship in the neighbourhood.

### St. Silas's Church

[Sunday services at 10.45 and 6.30; Hymnal Companion],

is in *St. Silas' Square*, on the west side of *Church Street*, nearly half a mile to the west of the Six Ways. It is a Gothic cruciform edifice of red brick, built in 1845, at a cost of some £1,700. There is a **Wesleyan Chapel**, facing *George Street*, the "next turn" to the west; and in *St. Michael's Street*, at the top of *Soho Hill*, half a mile further westward, is **St. Michael's Church**, Handsworth [*Sunday services at* 8.0, 10.30, 3.30, *and* 7.0].

Turning southward from Six Ways, along *Alma Street*, we soon pass a *Board School*, on our right; and recross the *Hockley Brook*, which, a little to the west, runs beneath the northern portion of **Burbury Street Recreation Ground**, one of Birmingham's pleasant lungs. We now find that our thoroughfare changes its name to

*Summer Lane.* We are in the parish of St. Stephen, and soon, on our right hand, at the point where *Porchester* and *Geach Streets* join that along which we are travelling, we pass a **Baptist Chapel.** Turning to the left (eastward) along *Cowper Street*, a few steps further on, and passing a *Board School*, we reach *Newtown Row.* Facing us on the opposite side, at the corner of *St. Stephen Street* (at the other end whereof is the triangular **Walmer Recreation Ground**), we see—

### St. Stephen's Church.

[Sunday services at 10.45, 3.30, and 6.30 (on the first and third Sundays in the month, at 8.0 a.m. and midday; on the others, at 7.0 and 8.0 a.m.); Hymns Ancient and Modern.]

Consecrated in July, 1844, it is a Geometric Gothic cruciform structure, the turret whereof contains a bell. A *School* adjoins it; and a little to the south, also in Newtown Row, we find, at the corner of *Hatchett Street*, a **Wesleyan Chapel.**

*Lower Tower Street* (the second turning on the right) conducts us to—

### St. Nicholas's Church.

[Sunday services at 11.0 and 6.30 (at 8.0 a.m. on the first and third Sundays in the month); Hymns Ancient and Modern.]

This brick edifice of Lancet, or First Pointed, architecture, was consecrated in 1868; it has a large five-lighted east window and rose windows in the west gable, all in the Geometrical Decorated style. The church consists of a nave, aisles of equal length, and a shallow and badly proportioned chancel, projected into the nave, with a low stone enclosure wall, panelled and forming the base of a screen of carved oak. The nave arcade has circular stone piers, the capitals of which have square abacii and are boldly carved with leaves and flowers. The stone pulpit is of Early English design. There is a handsome stone reredos; and many of the windows are filled with stained glass, in memory of deceased parishioners.

Continuing our walk along Lower Tower Street, crossing Summer Lane, and going on westward, along *Tower*

*Street*, to its junction with *Great Russell* and *Hampton Streets* (almost half a mile to the west of St. Nicholas's Church), we reach—

## St. George's Church

[Sunday services at 10.45, 3.0, and 6.30 ; Church Hymns],

built in 1822. It was designed by Rickman and is of Decorated architecture, with a western square embattled and pinnacled tower, containing a clock and a peal of bells ; the tower is a hundred and fourteen feet high, and its elevated position renders it conspicuous from all parts of the neighbourhood. The nave has a lofty clerestory, surmounted by a battlement and pinnacles, in keeping with those of the tower. It is separated from the aisles by a richly moulded arcade, and from the chancel by a lofty arch. The tracery of the storied east window is charming and richly designed.

Hampton Street runs straight southward to the junction of Constitution Hill and Snow Hill with Summer Lane, about a hundred yards from the spot at which—

## The Old General Hospital

faces the last-named avenue. This, the chief of Birmingham's institutions for the relief of the sick poor, as it was the earliest, owes its commencement to the efforts of Dr. Ash, in perpetuation of whose benevolent exertions the district in which he lived has been named "Ashted" ; while his house (Hutton describes it as "sumptuous") has been converted into a church (**St. James's**, Great Brook Street).* The building of the hospital was commenced in 1766, and it was opened in 1779. In the first year, it did good work, upwards of three hundred patients being admitted, of whom only ten died ; and from that time to the present the institution has been well supported. The establishment of the Triennial Musical Festival (to which we have already adverted,

* Its alteration took place in 1791, when, says Hutton, "a cupola rose from the roof . . . a pulpit and pews rose within it, and it became a chapel."

in 1768, gave a great impetus to the hospital; and it has been increased from time to time. At its centenary, on the 29th of September, 1879, the committee suggested that the occasion should be marked by the establishment of a department for the treatment of chronic cases in some part of the suburbs of Birmingham where patients may enjoy the benefit of prolonged treatment and of the curative agencies of rest and pure air; and this suggestion has borne fruit in the establishment of the **Jaffray Suburban Hospital**, at Gravelly Hill, which was opened by the Prince of Wales in 1885. It was erected and presented to the authorities by Sir John Jaffray, the originator of the " Birmingham Daily Post." The hospital itself was then too small to fulfil its annually increasing requirements, and steps were soon taken to provide a larger building, more in keeping with the advances of modern discoveries; and in 1894 the foundation stone of the New General Hospital, a little to the east, was laid by the Duke and Duchess of York; and we shall next direct our steps to its site, visiting other public edifices on our way.

But first of all, let us take a walk (or a ride by tramcar) up *Constitution Hill* as far as the **General Cemetery**, at *Key Hill*, and the **Church of England Cemetery**, between *Vyse Street* and *Icknield Street*, a little to its south. The former, opened in 1856, is a favourite resting-place with Nonconformists; it is about eleven acres in extent, and has in its centre a mortuary chapel of Classical design. It is to a great extent excavated from the rock, which is requisitioned for the construction of catacombs. The Church of England Cemetery is of similar area; it was consecrated in 1848, having been laid out in pursuance of the provisions of an Act of Parliament, obtained two years previously. It contains a handsome Perpendicular church—**St. Michael's** (*which is used for service on Sundays*), built of white freestone, and consisting of nave, chancel, and tower, the latter surmounted by a graceful spire. Both cemeteries are nicely laid out, and both contain attractive monuments, some of them of superior merit. Between the two burial grounds is the goods station of the Great Western Railway.

The local **Assay Office** is at the eastern corner of Newhall and Charlotte Streets, a little to the west of the junction of Summer Lane, Snow Hill, and Constitution Hill; and—

### St. Paul's Church

[Sunday services at 10.45 and 6.30; Church Hymns]

is nearer at hand. It stands in the centre of *St. Paul's Square*, and was consecrated in 1779. It is a square Græco-Italian building of stone, with a spire at its west end. Its great window is filled with stained glass, by Francis Eginton. The churchyard has been laid out as a public garden.

Reaching *Snow Hill*, we cross the *Birmingham and Fazeley Canal*, and then take the first turning to the left, *Bath Street*, on the north side whereof is—

### St. Chad's Roman Catholic Cathedral.

[Sunday services at 7.30, 8.30, 9.30, 11.0, 3.0, 4.0, and 6.30.]

This Middle Pointed edifice, consecrated in 1838, is one of the finest ecclesiastical edifices in Birmingham, and was built from the designs of Pugin. Its exterior is very plain—in fact, almost without ornament. The walls are carried to a great height, and a vast roof of slate stretches across the nave and aisles. The material used is red brick—the windows are of stone. All is simple, plain, and severe, yet thoroughly picturesque, its two slender spires, a hundred and eighty feet high, adding greatly to the effect of the building. The interior is magnificent in its simplicity. Two rows of Pointed arches, nearly eighty feet high, divide the nave from the aisles; there is no clerestory, and the whole is covered by an open timber roof. A very elaborate and beautiful rood-screen divides the choir from the nave. The high altar has a baldacchino over it; and beneath it, is a shrine, containing the bones of St. Chad, Bishop of Lichfield (*circa* 670). The body of this bishop appears to have been concealed by some of the old Roman Catholic families from the time of the Reformation until it was placed in this church. The west door is large, deeply recessed, and divided in the centre; above it, is a noble window, the Geometrical tracery of which is justly admired. The gable, above the window, terminates in a cross. The pulpit is of carved oak, of the sixteenth, and the episcopal throne and stalls of the fifteenth century. The walls are richly decorated, and on them are a large number of paintings; and there are two organs in the cathedral. Beneath it, is a *Crypt*, dedicated to St. Peter; and opposite its western end, the Bishop's House, the residence of the bishop and clergy. The latter, "an almost perfect specimen of mediæval domestic architecture," was also designed by Pugin.

## St. Chad's Convent

is in *Whittall Street*, which runs off Bath Street, a few steps to the east. In the same street and nearly opposite the convent, is—

## St. Mary's Church.

[Sunday services at 10.45 and 6.30; for men only, on the first Sunday in the month, and for children, on the third, at 3.0; Hymnal Companion.]

This church, which stands in a small oäsis of greenery, was built in 1774 and restored in 1857 and 1872. It is of somewhat peculiar appearance. It is octagonal in form and of heavy Italian architecture; and on its western side is an equally peculiar tower, surmounted by a slender spire. The tower consists of three stages—the lower one is circular; the second, polygonal, with pilasters at its angles and a balustrade; and the top one is of different designs on its alternate sides.

Immediately to the south of the church, and occupying the entire block between St. Mary's Square and Steelhouse Lane, north and south, and between Whittall Street and Loveday Street, in the other direction, is—

## The New General Hospital,

to which we have already referred. It was, as we have seen, commenced in 1894, when the Duke of York laid the foundation stone, and its total cost is estimated at something like £206,000, of which Miss Ryland, who

THE NEW GENERAL HOSPITAL.

has done so much for the town, bequeathed £25,000,

and Mr. Wilkes, £20,000. Built from designs by Mr. William Henman, F.R.I.B.A., the edifice will be an exceedingly handsome one, built in what is described as the free Classic style, conceived in a Gothic spirit. The elevations will be distinctly pleasing in their treatment; and the number and size of the windows will give it a light and cheerful appearance, and betoken the presence of that thorough ventilation, so necessary for health and comfort. It is being constructed of red brick and terracotta, and its roofs will be covered with green slate. The chief entrance faces Steelhouse Lane, whence the gates and porter's lodge will lead into a quadrangle, with buildings upon three sides. The structure is to consist of a central administrative block, connected, by covered cloisters, with two wings—one on either hand. Two main blocks will project from the corridors to the limits of the site facing St. Mary's Square; and the whole edifice will be three storeys high. At the junction of the cloisters and wings, there are to rise two lofty and handsome water towers, with pyramidal roofs; and smaller turrets, similar in design will ornament the angles of the building. It will provide accommodation for about three hundred in-patients, in addition to a theatre and the necessary apartments for the medical staff and nurses and rooms for the use of out-patients. Special provision for the treatment of children is to be made near Whittall Street; and the nurses' home, on the same side of the edifice, will be detached from the main building, access from the one to the other whereof will be attained by means of a covered corridor. The hospital will be lighted by electricity, and water is to be supplied from an artesian well, whence it will be pumped to cisterns in the towers.

*Steelhouse Lane* connects the north-eastern end of Corporation Street with Colmore Row; and the front of the hospital abuts on the eastern extremity of the lane, immediately opposite the rear of the Victoria Law Courts. Journeying westward, we pass—on the left (south) side of the street—

### Ebenezer Chapel

[Sunday services at 10.45 and 6.30],

one of the chief sanctuaries of the Congregational body in Birmingham. It was built, in 1817-18, to accommodate the large congregations, attracted by the preaching of the Rev. Jehoiada Brewer, who however did not live to see it completed.

Next we notice, also on our left, the out-patient department of the **Children's Hospital**, erected in 1867-8, from designs by Messrs. Martin and Chamberlain, at a cost of £3,000. The indoor department — the hospital, *par excellence*—is situated in Broad Street. We shall visit it on a future occasion. And so, reaching once more the Great Western Railway Station, we end our second walk about the city, and separate for the day.

## A WALK WESTWARD.

MEETING at the foot of the Peel Statue, sufficiently early to insure our having a long day before us, we make our way along *Paradise Street*. We pass the *Birmingham and Midland Institute*, on our right, and the *Queen's College*, on the left—both of these we have already visited; and then we notice the home of the **Clef Club**, a musical association established in 1881. We soon reach the offices of the South Stafford Water Co., at the south-western extremity of the street, the end of which is a junction of Easy Row and Suffolk Street, a spacious thoroughfare, running almost due north and south. Adjoining these offices, is the **Old Wharf**, where the Wolverhampton and Birmingham and the Worcester and Birmingham Canals terminate. The office looks down Paradise Street; its somewhat singular front is ornamented by a clock, and its door is approached by a double flight of steps, which, it is said, John Wesley once used as a pulpit.

The Curzon Hall, in Suffolk Street, where the annual dog shows take place and other meetings are held, is of Gothic architecture and composed of plain and coloured bricks, ornamented with stone work.

We turn to the north for a few yards, along *Easy Row*, a noteworthy feature whereof is the Homœopathic Hospital and Dispensary (this part of the city is tunnelled by the London and North-Western Railway, and it is well to remember that the tramcar is unknown in the streets we are about to traverse), and soon reach *Broad Street*, which runs to the west. We see the Dental Dispensary on the north (right-hand) side of the street; and not many steps further—

## The Prince of Wales Theatre,

the front of which, true to the commercial instincts of the city, is used as a row of handsome shops. The theatre has had a chequered career. It was built in 1856, as a music hall, and intended for the performance of high-class productions; but not proving very successful in that *rôle*, it was, in 1862, licensed as a theatre, the name being adopted as a commemoration of the wedding of the Prince in that year, and it was almost entirely reconstructed in 1876. Its interior is bright and cheerful.

## Bingley Hall,

behind the theatre, was constructed, by the alteration of Bingley House, the old seat of the Lloyds, as the site of the Exhibition of the Manufactures of Birmingham and the Midland Counties (the precursor, on a small scale, of the "World's Fair" of 1851) in 1849. Since then, the hall has been the scene of numerous political and social gatherings, and it is annually used for the cattle and poultry shows. St. Peter's Roman Catholic Church and the Convent of the Sisters of Notre Dame are in *St. Peter's Place.*

To the west of St. Peter's Place, the side of the building abutting on it, is—

## The Church of the Messiah

[Sunday services at 11.0 and 6.30],

belonging to the Unitarians. It is a picturesque structure, of Geometrical Gothic architecture; and is built on arches over the Wolverhampton Canal, the level of the waters whereof, as is usual with artificial streams, is changed by means of locks. It was designed by Mr. J. J. Bateman. Its west front is very ornate; it consists of a triple arcaded entrance, with granite columns, having foliated capitals, supporting richly moulded arches. Above these, is a large, five-light, traceried window, surmounted by a gable. On each side, are towers, one of which at the south-west angle is surmounted by a lofty spire. The sides of the church are ornamented by gables.

Still walking along the north side of the road, we pass the **English Presbyterian Church** [*Sunday services at 11.0 and 6.30*], erected, in 1848, on the site of a smaller one, built in 1834. It is of Italian architecture, with a tower, and is lighted from the roof. Next, we reach—

## The Children's Hospital,

at the corner of *Sheepcote Street*. When it was first established in 1861, the premises of the Polytechnic Institution, in Steelhouse Lane, were adapted to its requirements. But in 1869, soon after the opening of the last-named department, the building now before us—rendered vacant by the removal of the Lying-In Hospital to Newhall Street—was purchased, a handsome entrance and boundary railing was erected at the joint expense of Dr. Heslop and Mr. C. E. Mathews, and other alterations and improvements were made; and the in-patient department was removed hither. A wing, set apart and specially designed for infectious cases, was built in 1875. Pleasant grounds, gay with flowers and bright with the sheen of grassplots, face the street; and the hospital is one of the brightest buildings in the neighbourhood. Its funds are considerably assisted by the collections in the various Sunday schools in the city and neighbourhood.

On the opposite side of the way, near the corner of *Bishopsgate Street*, is **Immanuel Church** [*Sunday services at* 11.0 *and* 6.30; *Hymnal Companion*], built in 1865, from designs by Mr. E. Holmes. It is described as "a

CHURCH OF THE MESSIAH.

neat little structure," and of Decorated architecture. A "short quarter of a mile" to the east, and we reach—

### The Five Ways,

another of those open spaces of which we have already

spoken, in the centre whereof is a marble **Statue of Joseph Sturge**, the eminent philanthropist, famous for his exertions in the cause of negro emancipation. It is twenty-four feet high (including the pedestal), and represents Mr. Sturge, standing, with one hand resting on a Bible, and the other extended towards a sitting figure of Peace. The latter occupies a shoulder of the pedestal to his left hand, and one of Charity is similarly placed on his right, these two virtues being the chief characteristics of Mr. Sturge. Fountains and flowers complete the pleasing *tout ensemble*. It is from the chisel of Mr. John Thomas, the sculptor of Attwood's statue, cost £1,000, and was unveiled in 1862.

The Five Ways is so called because five wide thoroughfares radiate from it. We reached the spot by Broad Street, from the east; Hagley Road continues the line of street westward; Calthorpe Road runs to the south, Islington Row to the south-east, and Ladywood Road to the north. Harborne Road branches off westward between Hagley and Calthorpe Roads, and, changing its name to Augustus Road, Woodbourne Road, and Meadow Road, on its way, eventually becomes absorbed in the line of roads, leading to Hagley.

We shall continue our journey westward by Hagley Road, and then, returning to the Five Ways, make our way southward by Calthorpe Road, and so get a good idea of the characteristic features of Edgbaston, the "West-end" of Birmingham. But before doing so, we would make two *détours* to examine some of the interesting features of the neighbourhood. *Ladywood Road*, will conduct us to **Rotton Park Reservoir**, in which the Wolverhampton Canal stores its supply of water. It is one of the largest artificial sheets of water near the city.

### Summerfield Park

behind it, one of the large breathing spaces, belonging to the citizens of Birmingham, is more than thirty-four acres in area. It was purchased by the corporation in 1875 and opened by the Mayor, Mr. Alderman Baker, on the 2nd of June, 1876. This park, small at first, has been twice enlarged by the purchase of land. It has cost about £25,000; and it is, indeed, a charming recreation ground.

In *Summerfield Crescent*, between the park and the reservoir, is the **Lea Memorial Church**—*Christ Church, Summerfield*, to give it its correct ecclesiastical title—[*Sunday services at* 11.0 *and* 6.30; *Church Hymns*], a Perpendicular edifice, constructed of Derbyshire stone, with Bath stone dressings. It was built in 1833-4, as a memorial of a deservedly popular vicar of St. George's, Edgbaston.

*Islington Row* changes its names to *Great Colmore Street*, and connects the Five Ways with Bristol Street, along which we shall walk by and bye. About a hundred yards from the Five Ways, *Bath Row* branches off on the left, and conducts us to the gates of—

## The Queen's Hospital,

opened in 1841, mainly through the exertions of Mr. Sands Cox. It is under the patronage of her Majesty. The building consists of a centre with an elegant portico, surmounted by the arms of the Rev. Dr. Warneford (a great benefactor to the hospital), and two wings, known as the Victoria and Adelaide wings, with detached fever wards. In 1873, a new building, for the use of the out-patients, with laundry and mortuary, was erected, at a cost of £10,000, a considerable portion of which was raised by subscriptions among the working classes, augmented by a gift from the Queen. The old and new buildings are connected by a conservatory, used by the patients as a promenade; and there are recreation grounds for the convalescents. The *Chapel*, a more recent addition, has a handsome stained window of three lights, the subject whereof is "Christ Healing the Sick," presented by Mr. Jackson, of Bath Row. The hospital, which is entirely free, contains one hundred and twenty beds, which are used for the reception of accidents and urgent medical and surgical cases.

At the extreme east end of Bath Row, is—

## St. Thomas's Church

[Sunday services at 11.0 and 6.30; at 3.30, on the second Sunday in the month, for men only],

commenced in 1829 from the designs of Messrs. Rickman and Hutchinson. It is in the Greek-Ionic style of architecture. At its west end, in a semicircular portico, supported by Ionic columns, from which rises a quadrangular tower. The tower is surmounted by an octagonal cupola and a gilt star.

At Five Ways, we reach—

## Edgbaston,

a parish entirely included in the city. It is the residence of "them that's rich and high"—the merchant-princes of Birmingham. Though but a short distance from the Town Hall, it has preserved its semi-rural appearance to such an extent as to make it difficult to believe that one is so near (at the Five Ways barely a mile from it) the heart of a large manufacturing centre, and surrounded on all sides by hives of industry. The visitor is charmed by its park-like and picturesque beauty ; and gazes with rapture on the sights which greet him on every side.

## The Edgbaston Grammar School,

a branch of King Edward's School in New Street, rears its handsome façade in Hagley Road, within a few yards of the Sturge Statue. Built in 1838, as the Birmingham and Edgbaston Proprietary School, it is an Elizabethan edifice of red brick, with stone dressings, quite in keeping with the pretty residences by which it is surrounded. In 1883, it underwent considerable change, to adapt it to modern ideas of what a large grammar school should be ; and it now provides accommodation for the instruction of three hundred and fifty boys.

At the corner of *Francis Road*, on our right hand, about a hundred yards from Five Ways, we pass the **Edgbaston Assembly Rooms** ; and walking for a few yards up the street, reach—

## The Edgbaston Congregational Church

[Sunday services at 11.0 and 6.30],

erected in 1855, and intended as a memorial of the jubilee of the ministry of the celebrated John Angell James, at Carr's Lane Chapel, he himself laying the foundation stone. As our engraving shows, it is a handsome stone building of Geometric-Decorated architecture; its tower, of Bath stone, is eighty-six feet high, and it is surmounted by an octagonal spire, which rises to a height of eighty-four feet, in addition.

ST. THOMAS'S CHURCH.

Continuing our walk along the Hagley Road, and passing *Plough and Harrow Road* (which derives its name from a well-known hostelry—the village inn, in Edgbaston's younger days), we reach—

## The Oratory of St. Philip Neri.

[Sunday services at 7.0, 8.0, 9.30, 11.0, 3.0, and 7.0.]

This church, erected by the monks in 1852, and "dedicated to our Blessed Lady, under the title of her Immaculate Conception," is closely connected with Cardinal Newman who lived there for more than a quarter of a century and who breathed his last within its walls. Externally it is a plain building in the Italian style; the interior, however, is as ornate as are most of the sanctuaries of the "old church."

Passing *Wyndham Road*, we find a Baptist Chapel, at the west corner of its junction with our road; and *St. Augustine's Road*, in the western portion of Hagley Road, conducts us to St. Augustine's Church [*Sunday Services at* 8.30, 11.0, 3.45, *and* 6. 30; *Hymns Ancient and Modern*]. This modern church (consecrated on October 2, 1868), is a handsome Gothic structure of stone, with a tower and spire, a hundred and eighty-five feet high. There is some good modern stained glass in the east window.

A walk up *Monument Road* (which communicates with the *Monument Road Railway Station*) will enable us to visit St. John's Church [*Sunday services at* 7.0, 8.0, 11.0, 3.15 (*children's*), 4.0 (*men's*), *and* 6.30; *Hymns Ancient and Modern*], consecrated in 1852. It is a cruciform edifice of Decorated architecture, with a tower and short spire at its south-west angle.

*Vicarage Road*, which branches (southward) out of Hagley Road, immediately opposite the spot whence Monument Road runs away northward, crosses *Harborne Road*,* and conducts us to the principal gates of—

## The Botanical Gardens,

the property of the Birmingham Botanical and Horti-

* The most convenient means of reaching the Botanical Gardens from the centre of the city would be by "catching" a Harborne Road omnibus near the Town Hall—*fare, twopence;* but we have adopted this route for the sake of preserving the continuity of our "parable."

cultural Society. Opened in 1820, they form a most delightful retreat and are largely resorted to. They are some twelve acres in extent, and are beautifully laid out,

CONGREGATIONAL CHURCH, EDGBASTON.

with terraced walks, undulating lawns, and gay parterres. The gardens contain an arboretum, rosarium, pinetum, ferneries, and so forth; and its elliptical conservatory takes rank among the finest in Great Britain. *The charge for admission on Mondays is twopence each; on special days, from one to two shillings, according to circumstances; on ordinary days, other than Monday, sixpence.*

*Westbourne Road,* which skirts the northern railings of the gardens, reaches, a little to the east, the junction of *Calthorpe Road* and *Church Road,* where stands, about half a mile to the south of the Five Ways—

## St. George's Church.

[Sunday services at 11.0, 3.30, and 6.30; Hymns Ancient and Modern.]

It was built in 1838, and is a type of Early English architecture, rarely seen, but very beautiful. The west, and principal, entrance is by a pedimented doorway, beneath a lofty triplet, above which is a round window, surmounted by a gable and cross. At the angles are boldly projecting buttresses, supporting tall richly-worked pinnacles. The chancel was added in 1856; it is in keeping with the rest of the building, and is surmounted by a spirelet. Four stained glass windows were unveiled in 1888, on the fiftieth anniversary of the consecration of the church.

Turning southward, along Church Road, we next visit—

## The Deaf and Dumb Asylum,

opened in 1815; its fittings were presented by Lord Calthorpe. Since then, it has received increased support from benevolent individuals; and it has been from time to time enlarged, so that it now contains nearly two hundred children. It is supported by subscriptions, supplemented by annual payments by the friends of the children educated within its walls.

Crossing the Midland Railway and the Worcester Canal, we next reach—

## The Blind Asylum,

the front whereof faces *Carpenter Road,* running eastward from that along which we are travelling. (There is a station, just opposite the asylum, so that the return to New Street is easy and quick.) The institution was commenced in 1846; and its present home, a good specimen of Elizabethan architecture, was opened in 1852. A gymnasium, &c., was added in 1893 and opened by the Countess of Dudley. Church Road leads us to—

## St. Bartholomew's Church.

[Sunday services at 11.0 and 6.30; on the second, fourth, and fifth Sundays in the month, at 8.30; on the last (for children), at 3.30; Hymns Ancient and Modern.]

This, the parish church of Edgbaston, presents an appearance of age to which it has no claim. It stands on the site of a building dating from 777, of which a portion of the tower is all that remains. The edifice fared so badly during the storms which ushered in the Commonwealth that it was found necessary to rebuild the nave at the Restoration; and it was altered in 1810 to an extent which almost amounted to rebuilding. Since then,

ST. BARTHOLOMEW'S, EDGBASTON.

additions have been made to it from time to time to meet the growing requirements of the parishioners. It is an Early English edifice, with a low embattled western tower. The church contains several monuments of the Calthorpe family, and the churchyard is crowded with monuments of the dead. Elihu Burritt speaks of the church as—

"One of the most beautiful little churches in England. Its beauty is not in architectural proportions or pretensions, but in the charm which Nature has given to it. In the first place, it is picturesquely situated under the eaves of a stately grove that veils Edgbaston Hall, and its park and pool, from the road. Then it is completely netted, to the very top of its tower, with ivy. Hardly a square inch of its bare walls can be seen at a few rods' distance. No garden summer-house or bower could be greener from bottom to top. Robed thus by Nature in the best vestment she could weave for a sanctuary, it seems to have a more sacred consecration to the worship of God than an archbishop could give it. . . . In the little churchyard, which looks like a hopefully sculptured door-step of eternity, sleeps the dust of a sister of Washington Irving, who was the wife of one of the fathers of the town—the Venerable Henry Van Wart."

Adjoining the church, are—

## Edgbaston Hall and Park.

Of old, when the lords of the soil built their "stately homes," they usually placed the parish church near them; and Edgbaston was no exception to the rule. The hall is close to the church, in the north-eastern corner of the park. It occupies the site of an ancient building, for generations the seat of the lords of the manor and burnt at the Revolution of 1688 to prevent its sheltering Catholics. The present edifice has no special beauty of its own; constructed of brick, it was erected by Sir Richard Gough. The park is spacious, pleasant, and well timbered; and it contains **Edgbaston Pool**, frequented by waterfowl and, in frosty weather, a favourite resort of skaters.

From the church, *Priory Road* conducts us, past the site of the ancient Priory, now a gentleman's residence, across *Bristol* and *Pershore Roads*, to *Edgbaston Road*.

The latter, crossing the little river *Rea*, leads to the entrance to—

### Cannon Hill Park.

Birmingham owes this beautiful park (it has an area of fifty-seven acres), in common with so many of its public institutions, to the liberality of Miss Ryland. She presented it to the corporation in 1873; it is valued at more than £30,000. Considered one of the most beautiful of Birmingham's parks, it was tastefully laid out by Mr. Gibson, of Battersea; and it contains three lakes (one of which is used for boating purposes, while in another a bathing place has been constructed), cricket and croquet grounds, &c. It is bounded on the west by the Rea.

It may be well here to note that there are no less than eight free parks belonging to the corporation; and that the oldest of them only dates from 1856. Together, these grounds cover an area of nearly two hundred acres; and for two of them, whose united acreage is more than half that of the whole of Birmingham's lungs, the citizens are indebted to the liberality of Miss Ryland. Six years after her gift of Cannon Hill Park, she presented a second park (the second largest of the eight) to the town. It was originally known as *Small Heath Park*, but it was rechristened, in connection with a visit of Queen Victoria in the Jubilee year of her reign, as—

### Victoria Park.

It is situated on the Coventry Road, in the south-east portion of the city, and it is over forty-one acres in extent. It is valued at £30,000, and the donor contributed £4,000 in cash towards the cost of laying it out. It contains a large boating pool, with two small islands, where a number of waterfowl are kept. There is an excellent carriage drive round the park; and an ornamental refreshment pavilion has been erected upon an eminence commanding extensive views. It may be reached by tramcar, and there is a railway station close to it.

### Highgate Park,

in the Moseley Road, eight acres in area, was opened in 1876. Its chief feature is a large asphalted playground for children.

## The County Cricket Ground,

to the north of Edgbaston Road, occupies the greater

VICTORIA PARK: ENTRANCE GATE.

part of a small island, surrounded by the two branches of the Rea, which unite at its most northern point; and a short distance to the north-east is—

## Calthorpe Park,

approached from the *Pershore Road*. It is thirty-one acres in area, and was presented to the city by Lord Calthorpe. It was opened by the Duke of Cambridge in 1857; and its flat surface makes it serve admirably as a drill ground, for which purpose it is largely used by the local volunteers. The Rea runs along its eastern side.

Leaving the park, *Speedwell Road* will enable us to reach *Bristol Road*. After proceeding for about half a mile to the north—at the point where the road becomes *Bristol Street* and *St. Luke's Road*, a wide and important artery, runs away eastward—we reach another interesting group of public edifices. At the south-eastern corner of the junction of these two roads, is—

## Wycliff Chapel

[Sunday services at 11.0 and 6.30],

the most beautiful of the Baptist places of worship in Birmingham. It was designed by Mr. Cranston, and is of Fourteenth Century architecture. The edifice is of stone, and is described as a "parallelogram, with nave and aisles, and a tower and spire at the north-west angle." To the level of the roof, the tower is square; and then it becomes octagonal and is surrounded with clustered pinnacles and flying buttresses. The spire is richly crocketted and reaches an altitude of a hundred and forty feet. Both externally and internally, the chapel is beautifully ornamented, a statuette of Wycliffe being placed in the tympanum of the arch of the principal entrance. Above it, is a large traceried window, and the gable is surmounted by a cross. The elliptical baptistery is at the east end. It is entered below a large moulded archway, with detached shafts and enriched capitals. It is raised a few steps above the level of the nave; and is constructed of marble and paved with encaustic tiles. The pews and other fittings are in keeping with the architecture of the edifice.

At the other corner of the junction, there stands—

## St. Luke's Church.

[Sunday services at 11.0, 3.15, and 6.30 ; on the second Sunday in the month at 9.0 am. ; Hymns Ancient and Modern.]

This church, of which Mr. Harvey Egginton was the architect, was built in 1842; it is Norman in design, and has a tower at the south-west corner. The Licensed Victuallers' Asylum, erected in 1848-9, from designs by Mr. D. R. Hill, is the third of this group of edifices.

## The Old Meeting Church

[Sunday services at 11.0 and 6.30],

a little farther to the north, now belonging to the Unitarians, is the successor of the first place of worship erected by Dissenters in Birmingham. It is the substitute of the Old Meeting House removed a few years ago for the extension of New Street Station. The original building was destroyed in the "Church and King" riots of 1791, when the New Meeting House, of which Dr. Priestley was the minister, and several houses —those of Hutton and Dr. Priestley, amongst others —were wrecked. Dr. Priestley's valuable library, containing many priceless manuscripts, was burnt and his laboratory destroyed; and the town was in a state of anarchy for several days. The two meeting houses were rebuilt in a way "calculated to stand a siege," the Old Meeting House being opened in 1796, and the other in 1802; but in 1862 the latter was found insufficient for the wants of the congregation, and the Church of the Messiah, as we have seen was built in its stead.

Still walking northwards, we note a *Board School*, on our left; and our artery having become *Horse Fair*, we have the Roman Catholic Church of St. Catherine of Sienna, consecrated in 1875, on the same side. Soon afterwards the main road becomes *Suffolk Street*, and leads us to Paradise Street, where we commenced our walk. Facing Suffolk Street, on the right, just to the north of *Navigation Street*, is—

## The Technical School,

a strong and well-built edifice, yet ornamented withal. It

is composed of brick, with pressed facings and terra-cotta dressings, cornices, mouldings, &c., and it has an iron balcony railway, with wrought-iron escape ladders, so as

WYCLIFFE CHAPEL.

to provide the means of exit from the upper floors, in case of fire, without having recourse to the stairs. The main entrance from Suffolk Street, leads through a handsome hall, in which is the curator's office. The edifice consists of three floors, to each of which are two staircases, connected by corridors, communicating, on the basement level, with the open yard, from which a gateway leads into Summer Street, in the rear. This forms a special means of exit in case of emergency. The building contains lecture rooms, teachers' rooms, an examination room, a library, class rooms and workshops, and everything necessary for the proper working of the school.

From the south of Suffolk Street, *John Bright Street* runs off to the north-east and connects with *Hill Street*, which links New Street and the Pershore Road.

The northern portion of Hill Street is bounded by the **London and North-Western and Midland Railway Station**; and on its opposite side, a little to the south, is St. Jude's Church [*Sunday services at* 10.45 *and* 6 30], a modern structure (it was consecrated in 1851) of red brick, in the Early English style. There are a *Music Hall*, a number of chapels and schools, some public baths, and so forth in the neighbourhood. Perhaps as interesting as any of them, standing on *Singer's Hill, Blucher Street*, to the west of Suffolk Street, is—

### The Jewish Synagogue.

[Sabbath (Saturday) services at 8.45 and sunset.]

This, the fourth synagogue the Jews have had in Birmingham, was opened in 1856. It was designed in the Byzantine style, by Mr. Yeoville Thomason, and is a beautiful and commodious building.

\*     \*     \*     \*     \*

And here we bring our Walks about Birmingham to a close. We might easily multiply them, the more especially as, in every direction, we should meet with edifices of sufficient interest to merit detailed descriptions; but those along which we have accompanied our friends will be sufficient for our purpose, for they have shown us the nature of the street architecture of the city.

## Charitable Institutions, Hospitals, &c.

The charitable institutions of Birmingham are numerous, though but few of them demand an extended notice. The following are the chief of them, the figures indicating the date when they were opened:—

*Almshouses—*
  *Glover's (Mrs.)*, Steelhouse Lane; 1826.
  *James's (Misses)*, at Nechells.
  *Lench's*, Conybere Street, Hospital Street, Ravenhurst Street, and Ladywood Road; 1539, &c.
  *Lloyd's*, Belgrave Street; 1869.
  *Sir Josiah Mason's;* 1858.
*Birmingham and Midland Free Hospital for Sick Children*, Broad Street.
*Birmingham District Nursing Society*,
*Birmingham Medical Mission*, Floodgate and River Street; 1875.
*Children's Emigration Homes*, St. Luke's Road; 1872.
*Children's Hospital*, Broad Street; established in 1861; out-door department, Steelhouse Lane.
*Crowley's Orphanage for Poor Girls*, 43 and 44, Lee Crescent, Edgbaston.
*Deaf and Dumb Asylum*, Edgbaston; 1815.
*Ear and Throat Infirmary*, 109, Edmund Street; 1844.
*Eye Hospital*, Church Street; 1823.
*General Dispensary*, Union Street; 1793. Branches at Highgate, Nechells, Ladywood, and Lozells.
*General Hospital*, Summer Lane; 1766.
*General Institution for the Blind*, Carpenter Road, Edgbaston; 1852.
*Homœopathic Hospital*, 15, Easy Row; 1875; commenced in 1845.
*Hospital for Women*, Spark Hill; 1878; out-door department, Upper Priory.
*Jaffray Suburban Branch of the General Hospital*, Gravelly Hill; 1885.
*Ladies' Association for the Care of Friendless Girls* (Mrs. Roger's Memorial Home), St. Vincent Street, Ladywood.
*Ditto for the Care and Protection of Young Girls;* training home, 66 and 67, Summer Hill.
*Licensed Victuallers' Asylum*, Bristol Street; 1848.
*Lying-In Charity*, 71, Newhall Street; 1842.
*Magdalen Asylum*, Clarendon Road, Edgbaston.
*Mason's (Sir J.) Orphanage*, Erdington; 1858.
*Medical Benevolent Society*, 33, Paradise Street; 1821.
*Moseley Hall Convalescent Home for Children;* 1892.
*Orthopædic and Spinal Hospital*, Newhall Street; 1817.
*Princess Alice Orphanage*, New Oscott.
*Queen's Hospital*, Bath Row; 1840.
*Reformatory for Boys*, Saltley; 1852.
*Servants' Home and Register Office for Nurses*, Bath Row.
*Skin and Lock Hospital*, John Bright Street; 1880.
*Society for the Relief of Infirm Aged Women;* 1825.
*Working Boys' Home*, Gordon Hall, 18 to 20, Deritend.

## Educational Institutions, Schools, &c.

In addition to those founded by the School Board and other elementary schools, the following are among the chief educational institutions in the town:—

*Birmingham and Midland Institute*, Paradise Street; 1855.
*Birmingham Certified Industrial School*, Gem Street.
*Blue Coat School*, Colmore Row; 1722.
*Bourne College*, Quinton Park, Quinton; 1882.
*Bridge Trust School*, Handsworth.
*Certified Industrial Schools*, Penn Street, Deritend.
*Congregational Training College*, Moseley; 1838. *(See "Moseley.")*
*Edgbaston Church of England College for Girls*, Calthorpe Road.
*Edgbaston Grammar School*, Five Ways; originally the Birmingham and Edgbaston Proprietary School; erected, 1838; adapted as a Grammar School by the Governors of King Edward's Foundation, 1883.
*Edgbaston High School for Girls*, 24, Hagley Road.
*Edgbaston Preparatory School for Boys*, Hagley Road.
*Grammar School, King Edward's*, New Street; 1552.
*Handsworth Commercial School*, Soho Hill.
*Hebrew National Schools*, Ellis Street.
*King Edward's Grammar Schools*, Bath Row, Camp Hill, Summer Hill, and Frederick Road, Aston.
Ditto—Girls, Congreve Street.
*King's Heath Institute School*, Alcester Road; 1878.
*Municipal School of Art*, Margaret Street; 1885.
*Municipal Technical School*, Bristol Street; erected, 1894.
*Protestant Dissenting Charity School*, Graham Street; 1760.
*Queen's College*, Paradise Street; 1828.
*Saltley Training College*; 1874. *(See "Saltley.")*
*St. Edmund's College for Boys*, St. Edmund's Street.
*St. Mary's Roman Catholic College*, Oscott; 1837-8. *(See "Oscott.")*
*Sir Josiah Mason's Science College*, Edmund Street; 1880.
*Society of Friends Priory School*, Upper Priory.
*Wesleyan Theological College*, Handsworth; 1880.

## Cemeteries.

There are three public cemeteries in Birmingham. The **General Cemetery**, on Key Hill, opened in 1836, a picturesque "God's acre" and favourite resort of the townsfolk; the **Church of England Cemetery**, Warstone Lane, consecrated in 1848, the handsome Perpendicular church of which is used for public services (*see* "St. Michael's"); and the **City Cemetery**, at Witton, the property of the corporation. **St. Joseph's Catholic Cemetery**, Thimble Mill Lane, is about five acres in area, and contains a convent with chapel, presbytery, and schools; and the **Jews' Burial Ground** is in Islington Road.

## Public Parks and Recreation Grounds.

Birmingham is well provided with "breathing spaces" for the masses, while the railways bring within easy reach of all many places of historic interest with which the neighbourhood abounds. In addition to the cemeteries, which, on account of the taste displayed in laying them out, and in the monuments with which they are adorned, may almost be classed among them, there are no less than eight free parks belonging to the corporation, the oldest of which only dates from 1856. Together, these grounds cover an area of over two hundred acres; and the corporation obtained possession of an extensive tract of land, known as the *Lickey* and situated on the Rednall and Bilberry Hills, in Worcestershire, and threw them open to the public in 1888. The parks are open from six in the morning until sunset between March 31st and September 30th; and during the other portion of the year, from sunrise to sunset.

*Adderley Park*, Saltley; 10 acres; 1856. *(See* "Saltley.")
*Aston Park and Hall*; 1858. *(See* "Aston.")
*Balsall Heath Park*; 5 acres.
*Burbury Street Recreation Ground*; a present from Mr. William Middlemore in 1877; 4½ acres.
*Calthorpe Park*, Pershore Road; 1857; 31½ acres.
*Cannon Hill Park*; 1873; 57¼ acres.
*Highgate Park*, Moseley Road; 8¾ acres; 1876. Its chief feature is a large asphalted playground for children.
*Nechells Public Gardens*; 9 acres.
*Park Street Gardens* (the "Old Burial Ground); 1880; 4¼ acres.
*St. Mary's Gardens*; 1882; 2¾ acres.
*Summerfield Park*, Dudley Road; 1876; 34 acres.
*Victoria Park*, Small Heath; 1879; 43¼ acres.
*Walmer Recreation Ground*; 4¾ acres.

The **Cavalry Barracks**, built in 1793, are in Great Brook Street, Ashted.

## The Clubs

in the city are numerous ; among them are :—

*Clef Club*, Paradise Street.
*Conservative Club*, Temple Row.
*Liberal Club*, Lower Temple Street.
*Liberal Unionist Club*, Martineau Street.
*Midland Club*, Masonic Hall, New Street.
*Midland Conservative Club*, Waterloo Street.
*Midland Arts Club*, New Street.
*Union Club*, Colmore Row.

The **Workhouse**, in Western Road, was built in 1850-2, from designs by Mr. Bateman, and has since been enlarged under the supervision of Messrs. Martin and Chamberlain. It is an Elizabethan edifice, capable of housing two thousand inmates ; its chapel, in the Perpendicular style, has a bell turret and some stained-glass windows. The **City Hospital**, only separated from the Workhouse by a wall, dates from 1874.

The **Lunatic Asylum**, in Lodge Road, was opened in 1850, from the plans of Mr. D. R. Hill; it is of Early Tudor architecture and stands in the midst of about thirty-six acres in extent of ornamental grounds. An **Asylum for Chronic Cases**, at Rubery Hill, is of more recent construction.

The **Jail**, also designed by Mr. D. R. Hill, was opened in 1849. Constructed of brick, with stone dressings, and Romanesque in style, it is arranged upon the principal adopted at Pentonville, and the watch turrets, on the walls, give it quite a castellated appearance.

The **Fire Brigade Central Station** is in Upper Priory, and there are numerous branches "all over the place." It is well provided with engines and horses, pumps, fire-escapes, scaling-ladders, and everything else which a fire brigade should have ; and its *personnel* is not behind that of the metropolis itself. The brigade was originated in 1874, although before that several tentative efforts towards the establishment of the machinery for quelling the outbursts of the "fire fiend" had been made. Even as early as 1695, there is the record of the fact that a fire engine was in existence, and that one William Burn agreed to keep it "in order and to play it four times every yeare" for the sum of "twenty shillings a yeare." No doubt, it was a primitive affair—possibly as primitive as the spelling of the agreement—and when one notes the name of the engineer, one is inclined to think that it must have been adopted as a grim joke. But, whatever may have been the quality of the engine and the capability of the keeper thereof in 1695, its existence is a proof of the progressive tendencies of the inhabitants of Birmingham from the very commencement of the town; and if we are ever so unfortunate as to witness a conflagration on a large scale during our residence in the city, we shall be convinced that in the provision of men and means to cope with such a calamity, as in everything else, the authorities are abreast with, if not in advance of, those of other places.

THE GREAT GALLERY, ASTON HALL.

THE MINT, ICKNIELD STREET.

## THE TRADE AND MANUFACTURES OF BIRMINGHAM.

WE have already alluded to the "industries" of Birmingham, their effect upon its marvellous prosperity, and the interest which they afford to all visitors to the city. We will now devote a few pages to their consideration.

A marked peculiarity about the arrangements of the "toy shop of Europe" lies in its division into great "quarters," so to speak. In the triangle formed by New Street, High Street, Bull Street, and Colmore Row, and their immediate neighbourhood, are to be found, as we have seen, all the chief public buildings in the place; and the various "industries" of Birmingham are located almost entirely in separate and distinct parts of the town. Thus, the manufacturers of guns and pistols, and of all things connected therewith, have established themselves around St. Mary's Church. The jewellers are in the neighbourhood of St. George's and St. Paul's Churches; and the metal and button workers are to be found in other parts of the town. Another striking feature of the manufactures of the place lies in the fact that the whole of the work is not done in the large factories, as is the case elsewhere. Much of it is given out to "little masters"—persons employing a small number of boys, men, and girls (for female labour is largely utilised in the town). This arises from the immense subdivision of labour in the place. Many things, which appear to emanate from one workshop, have in reality passed through a score; and it is nothing unusual for the various portions of one piece of mechanism to be manufactured in different parts of the town, at a distance from one another, and only come together in the establishment of the firm who contracted with the customer for its production. Birmingham is so busy a place that it is said there is not a street, however small, without a manufactory and an engine, and that the whole town is honeycombed with workshops.

The city has always been famous for the number of the followers of Tubal-Cain to be found within her borders. We have seen that Leland and Camden both found "smithes and cutlers" there; and it is probable that, if the monks, with whom Hutton was so greatly displeased for their omission to do so, had left us any record of the Birmingham of their day, its most prominent feature would be the multitude of "artificers in brass and iron" dwelling in the town. But Hutton entertains a fond idea that they lived there, long before the days of "these religious drones," as he calls them; he thinks that the Ancient Britons obtained their swords and spears, their shields, and the scythe blades which armed their chariots from the town. It may have been so; but as history does not throw any light on the subject, it is impossible to speak about it with any degree of certainty.* This much we do know—that the more recent manufacture of swords was not introduced till the days of Charles I., when the inhabitants embarked in the enterprise in order to supply the Roundheads with the weapons they refused to sell to the Cavaliers; so that, if their ancestors exercised the art in those remote days, the knowledge of it had died out.

It was not till the Restoration that the modern era of its commerce can be said to have commenced. The introduction, by the famous Dud Dudley, of the system of smelting iron with coal had greatly benefited South Staffordshire; and Birmingham manufacturers were not slow in availing themselves of its advantages, at the time when the many branches of ornamental manufacture for which the town has since become noted began to be developed. Hutton, who wrote in the latter part of the eighteenth century, alluded to the anticipated effect of these changes in the quaint language in which he delighted. He said:—

"Though we have attended her [Birmingham] through so immense a space, we have only seen her in infancy, comparatively small in her size, homely in her person, and coarse in her dress; her ornaments wholly of iron from her own forge. But now her growth will be amazing, her expansion rapid, perhaps not to be paralleled in history. We shall see her rise in all the beauty of youth, of grace, and of elegance, and attract the notice of the commercial world. She will add to her iron ornaments, the lustre of every metal that the whole earth can produce, with all their illustrious race of compounds, heightened by fancy and garnished with jewels. She will draw from the fossil and the vegetable kingdoms; press the ocean for shell, skin, and coral. She will also tax the animal for horn, bone, and ivory; and she will decorate the whole with the touches of her pencil."

And time has proved that the old bookseller was right! When he wrote the discoveries of Watt were beginning to make a noise in the world. The works at Soho had

* "The data for this theory are rather thin and feeble; but there may be good basis of probability for it to rest upon. Whatever tools of labour or weapons of war were made of iron or copper by the Ancient Britons, might as well have been made at Birmingham and in its vicinity as anywhere else in the kingdom."—*Elihu Burritt.*

been but recently founded ; and there—and afterwards at Smethwick—Watt and his coadjutors, Boulton, Murdock, and Egginton, established great schools of mechanical engineering and matured inventions which have since "turned the world upside down." Of these, the chief was —as every schoolboy knows—the practical application of steam as a motive power for machinery ; while scarcely second to it was the elaboration of the system of artificial illumination by means of gas, which was "first set aglow in the Soho works, to celebrate the conclusion of peace between France and England in 1802." Birmingham steadily advanced through the momentous epoch of the nineteenth century ; she has fully earned the motto, "Forward," engraved on her civic seal. Year by year, new branches of manufacture have sprung into being, until at the present day the one feature of the industries of the place which strikes a stranger more than any other is their multiplicity and variety.

Everything that can be made of metal is made at Birmingham ; indeed, the ramifications of its industries are so numerous that it would be next to impossible to mention them all. At one time, its people possessed an unenviable reputation for the manufacture of counterfeit coin. We have read of Birmingham being named "the town of base coinage," but that is happily a thing of the past. Boulton established a **Mint**—at first only for the issue of copper coins—at Soho in 1778. It is described by Lewis as "of very ingenious construction. By it, with the assistance of only one person to supply it with the material and another to receive it when finished, the whole process of coining was performed from the rolled metal. From this mint, issued a great portion of the copper coinage of George III., all the silver Bank tokens of 1804, and numerous medals. . . . In this establishment, also, was adopted the first application of gas, as a substitute for oil and tallow, by Mr. Murdock, who, after a course of experiments at Redruth, in Cornwall, lighted the shops of this factory, and, in 1802, displayed the success of his researches in a splendid public illumination of the Soho, in celebration of the peace with France." The work is now carried on in Icknield Street, by The Mint, Birmingham, Limited, formerly Ralph Heaton and Sons. Money is made, not only for the British, but for a great many other governments too—the Emperor of China, in the east, and the South American republics, in the west, being among Birmingham's customers. Most of the coins struck here are known by a very small letter, H, generally to be found under the date. This letter represents the name, "Heaton," the founder of the present company. They are also large manufacturers of seamless brass and copper tubes, rolled metals, wire, rods, stampings, machinery for minting, and so forth.

**Messrs. Elkington and Co.'s Silver and Electro-plate Works**, in Newhall Street, should be visited by the tourist wishing to obtain some idea of the manufactures of Birmingham. The extensive premises are approached by a magnificent staircase, decorated at intervals with bronze statues of the knights who signed the Magna Charta, reproductions of those in the House of Lords, which were manufactured by this celebrated firm. The show-rooms are very extensive and highly ornamented, works of art being lavishly displayed. Statues, trophies, vases, &c., in gold, silver, and bronze, in most brilliant and dazzling combination, surround us on every side. Proceeding through the studios—where artists are seen engaged designing and modelling the costly works for which this firm is celebrated—the well-adapted and commodious workshops are at length reached. All are furnished with the most approved machinery and are extremely interesting. The big stamp worked by steam, an adaptation of the Nasmyth steam-hammer, can deliver a blow of prodigious force and yet be modulated so as barely to crack a hazel nut; with three blows, it will execute as much work as formerly took a workman a whole day to do. After seeing the whole process of manufacture, we reach the plating and gilding department, and here our attention is attracted by the thousands of articles suspended in the various vats, receiving their deposits of the rich materials; and a huge galvanic battery, pointed out to us, is sufficiently powerful to destroy a regiment of soldiers at one shock. The *Jasmine Vase*, of which we present our readers with an engraving, is one of the *chefs d'œuvres* of this noted house. Designed by M. Willms, their principal artist, it is a beautiful specimen of modelling and chasing, the large panels in front and back being finely damascened in gold. Another specimen of repoussé work is the charming *Lyre Vase*, a marvel of its kind, designed and executed by Mr. T. Spall, chief artist in repoussé in Messrs. Elkington's employ, and a disciple of the renowned artist, Morel Ladeuil. *The works, which may be viewed on presentation of card of introduction, are open between ten and half-past twelve and from half-past two till four o'clock.*

Perhaps, of all its industries, it is its invention and manufacture of Steel Pens ("the small arms of literature, business, and social intercourse," Burritt terms them) which has contributed more largely than any other to make the city famous among the *literati* of modern times. They were invented by a Sheffield knife cutler, who, together with a neighbour, a tinman, manufactured them in small quantities; but it is Mr. Joseph Gillott who must be considered the "father" of the trade, not only in Great Britain, but throughout the world. The process

THE JASMINE VASE.

of making steel pens, briefly stated, is as follows:—The steel from which the pens are made is cut into strips about four inches wide, which, after being dipped in oil, are rolled and rolled again, until they acquire the requisite thinness and consistency. The pen-making machines are much the same in every case—stamps worked either by the foot or by hand. By division of labour, the work is passed from hand to hand, different operatives undertaking the cutting out of the blanks from the sheet of steel, the making of the holes, the slits, and the grinding. Then follows the process of annealing, bronzing, &c. Messrs. **Gillott and Sons**, Perry, Mitchell (with the originators of which firm Gillott was associated for some time), **Brandauer, Heath**, and others are noted for their steel pens and for the improvement they have introduced into their construction.

Pins are made in Birmingham by the million; and the button industry of the town has furnished more than one interesting chapter in its history. In its palmy days, when buttons of gold and other metals were the rage, fortunes were built up from the profits arising from their production; but Fashion is proverbially fickle, and though a law was passed to render the use of cloth-covered buttons penal, she proved stronger even than an Act of Parliament. As a consequence, the trade languished; but of late horn and bone buttons have come extensively into use, so that the manufacture—originally introduced by John Taylor, who died in 1775—is still one of the staples of the place.

The casting of church bells has long been a *spécialité* among Birmingham's many industries, Messrs. Carr's works, at Smethwick, taking a foremost place among the foundries of the United Kingdom. Nearly akin to the bells are the "storied windows" of the sanctuaries; and this reminds us that the stained glass of the Hardmans and of Bourne is of European fame. The ornamental glass of Osler (whose crystal fountain was one of the great attractions of the Exhibition of 1851 and is still to be seen in the Sydenham Crystal Palace) and of Chance are almost as widely known. Tangye's hydraulic jacks are famous as having launched the Great Eastern and raised the Cleopatra Needle to its present position on the Thames Embankment. To the steam engines and boilers introduced by Watt, we have already alluded; but the modern bicycle should not be forgotten in the enumeration of Birmingham's industries, though Coventry is more famous for this particular "line" of metal work.

Printing, too, has had, and still has much to do with the prosperity of the place. [Can our readers instance any successful community that does not owe a great deal to the Press?] The "typographers" of to-day are by no means behind their brethren in other towns. In the past, Birmingham was famous as the home of the talented Baskerville; and the journals of the town are ably conducted, well printed, and a "power in the state." Baskerville was a self-made man. Originally, a stonemason by trade, he became a schoolmaster, a japanner, and lastly an eminent type-founder and printer, his great work being a large folio Bible, now scarce and costly.

The **Moor Street Printing Works**, belonging to Messrs. White and Pike, which were established in 1848, have for many years been celebrated for ornamental and colour printing. Work sent out by this establishment may be seen in every part of the United Kingdom and the Continent of Europe. In this and the various branches of general printing, account-book making, the manufacture of envelopes, and so forth, a great variety of costly and ingenious machinery is used and several hundred persons are employed. Tin printing and the manufacture of ornamental tin boxes is also largely carried on by the firm, who have recently erected new and extensive works for this branch of business at Longbridge, near Northfield (seven miles from the city) on the Midland Railway.

One of the most important additions to the industries of Birmingham is the manufacture of **Californian Borax** by the **Patent Borax Company, Ltd.**, whose works are located in Ledsam Street, Ladywood. This special kind of borax first reached England in 1873; and it was soon seen that it could be rendered so pure—and at the same time so cheap—that its antiseptic properties might be of great use in the promotion of personal as well as domestic cleanliness. In 1874, the company took steps to test the practicability of the idea; and they have carried it out so successfully that they have completely revolutionised the trade. They have discovered an infinite variety of uses for the borates—most of them never before dreamt of; and they have invented and patented costly machinery for adapting them to those purposes. The crude mineral is now advantageously prepared for toilet and domestic use, and is sold to the public in penny packets, with ample directions as to its application; and so efficacious is it found that it is becoming increasingly popular with all classes of the community. It is valuable for washing, cleansing, and purifying clothes and household requisites; for disinfecting purposes and sanitation; and to visitors to Birmingham and to tourists in general, the toilet preparations in which it forms the principal ingredient will be especially welcome. The perfumed "Beauty" borax, as it is appropriately named, not only softens the water (and it is on that account useful to travellers), but is invaluable in the lavatory, on account of the beneficial effect on the skin, the hair, &c. In the form of tooth-powder (known as the "Queen of Beauty"), too, it acts beneficially on the dental organs, prevents the accumulation of tartar, strengthens the gums, and sweetens the breath—a quality which makes it a favourite preparation with the youth of both sexes. It is also made into transparent soap tablets, the use whereof is a luxury; and, in this form, it is inclosed in dainty glass jars and supplied to gentlemen for shaving purposes, and is especially grateful to those troubled with sensitive skins.

The gold and silver work of Birmingham is sufficiently extensive to demand the establishment of a branch assay office;* and the Government has established the **Gun-**

\* Two million pounds' worth of the precious metals are annually used in the manufactories at Birmingham.

proof House in Banbury Street to test the quality of the small arms manufactured in the town. The bronze and ormolu works, the brass foundries, gasfitting manufactories, galvanized iron works, wire drawing, chemical works, papier-maché factories, and a host of other trades are of world-wide reputation. Guns, swords, and other weapons, too; jewellery and trinkets—good and inferior; saddlery and harness; lamps, copying presses, and other kinds of goods are but part of the products of Birmingham. It is literally true that in Birmingham—

> "Art's ponderous fabric reels
> Beneath machinery's ten thousand wheels.
> Loud falls the stamp; the whirling lathes resound;
> And engines heave, while hammers clatter round.
> What labour forges, patient Art refines,
> Till bright as dazzling day, metallic beauty shines."

# COBDEN HOTEL
## CORPORATION STREET,
## *BIRMINGHAM*

One Minute from New Street Railway Station. Three Minutes from Great Western Station.

**120 BEDROOMS.**

**PASSENGER LIFT.**

No Gratuities.     Telephone No. 251.

*Registered Telegraphic Address—"COBDEN," BIRMINGHAM.*

### Tariff.

|  | Single. | Double. |
|---|---|---|
| BED AND ATTENDANCE, per night, each person— |  |  |
| When one meal per day taken in hotel | 2/6 | 4/- |
| When no meal taken in hotel | 3/6 | 5/- |
| BREAKFAST OR TEA : Plain | 1/- |  |
| Ditto, with eggs, fish, meat, or poultry | 1/6 to 2/- |  |
| DINNERS : Soup, fish, joints, sweets, &c., or *à la carte* | 2/- |  |

Letters or telegrams addressed—

"THE MANAGERESS,"

COBDEN HOTEL.

# EXCELSIORS
## CANNOT BE EXCELLED
### FOR
## TOURING.

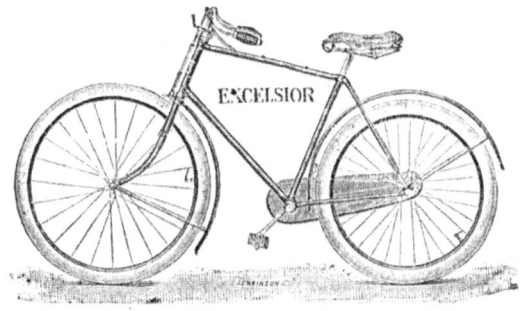

This Safety weighs 36 lb. as drawn, and is guaranteed for 13 stone.

WE ALSO MAKE

FRONT-DRIVING SAFETIES, TRICYCLES, TANDEMS, &c., &c.

*Lists and all needful information willingly supplied by*

## BAYLISS, THOMAS & CO.,
### COVENTRY.

Telegrams: "EXCELSIOR, COVENTRY."

*Railway Routes.*

# LONDON & NORTH-WESTERN RAILWAY.

## WEST COAST ROYAL MAIL ROUTE
BETWEEN
### ENGLAND AND IRELAND,
And between ENGLAND AND SCOTLAND.

### EXPRESS TRAIN SERVICES.

Liverpool (Lime St.) and London (Euston) in 4½ hours.
Manchester (London Rd.) ,, ,, 4¼ ,,
Chester ,, ,, 4 ,,
Birmingham (New Street) ,, ,, 2½ ,,
Glasgow (Central) ,, ,, 8¼ ,,
Edinburgh (Princes Street) ,, ,, 8½ ,,
Aberdeen ,, ,, 12 ,,
Dublin ,, ,, 10 ,,
Belfast ,, ,, 13¼ ,,

**Special Train Services** are in operation between WILLESDEN and VICTORIA, WILLESDEN and the CRYSTAL PALACE and CROYDON, and WILLESDEN and SOUTHALL, connecting with the Lines SOUTH of the THAMES.

**Train Services** are also in operation between WILLESDEN and KENSINGTON (for Waterloo and the London and South-Western Railway), and between WILLESDEN, BROAD STREET, KEW, and RICHMOND.

**Sleeping Saloons** by the night trains between London and Liverpool, London and Manchester, London and Holyhead, London and Edinburgh, Glasgow, Stranraer, and Perth; extra charge 5s. for each berth, in addition to the ordinary first-class fare.

**Dining Saloons** between London and Manchester, and London and Liverpool; Table d'Hote dinners, 3s. 6d. each.

**Corridor Trains** with **Refreshment** and **Dining Cars attached** for **1st** and **3rd Class passengers,** between London (Euston), and Edinburgh (Princes Street), and Glasgow (Central).

**Luncheon, Dinner,** and other **Refreshments,** served *en route.*

| **Luncheons.** | **Teas.** | **Dinner,** Table d'Hote. |
|---|---|---|
| 1st Class, 2/6. | Pot of Tea, | 1st Class, 3/6. |
| 3rd Class, 2/-. | Roll and Butter, 6d. | 3rd Class, 2/6. |

**Hotel Accommodation.**—LONDON (Euston Hotel), LIVERPOOL (North Western Hotel), BIRMINGHAM (Queen's Hotel), PRESTON (Park Hotel), CREWE (Crewe Arms), GLASGOW (Central Station Hotel), PERTH (Station Hotel), DUBLIN (North Western Hotel), HOLYHEAD (Station Hotel), GREENORE, BLETCHLEY, BLAENAU, FESTINIOG (North Western Hotel). The accommodation provided at these hotels is of the highest standard, and the charges will be found reasonable.

**Hot or Cold Luncheons** at all principal stations, 3s., including beer or wine, and 2s. 6d. without.

**Tourists' Arrangements, 1894.**—Tourist tickets are issued during the season (May 1st to October 31st) from the Company's principal stations to Scotland, the English Lake District, Ireland, North, South, and Central Wales, Malvern, Buxton, Stratford-on-Avon, Scarborough, Harrogate, Southport, Blackpool, Morecambe, Isle of Man, Isle of Wight, Jersey, and Guernsey.

Every information as to trains and fares can be obtained on application to Mr. G. P. Neele, Superintendent of the Line, Euston Station, London, N.W.

EUSTON STATION, 1894      FRED. HARRISON, *General Manager.*

LANCASTER'S "LADIES" CAMERA
(Patent), 42/-

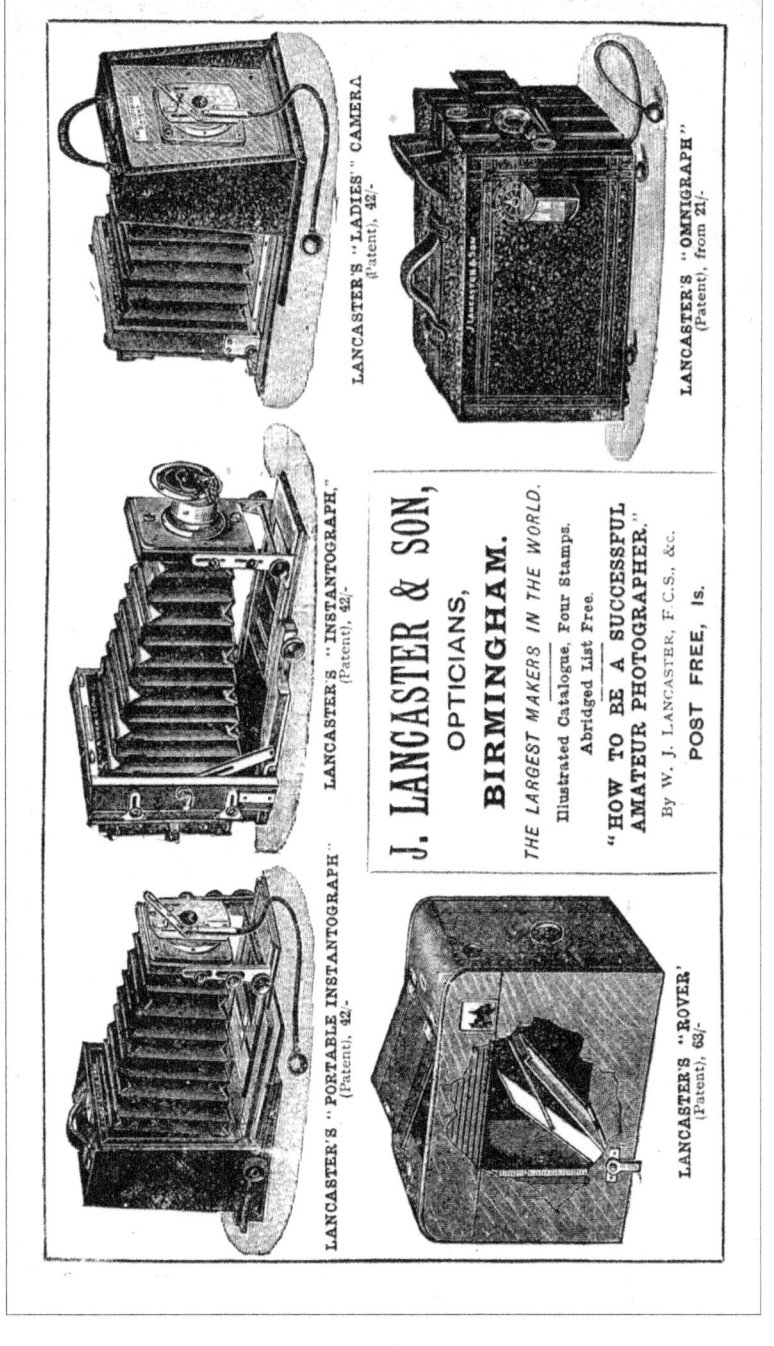

LANCASTER'S "OMNIGRAPH"
(Patent), from 21/-

LANCASTER'S "INSTANTOGRAPH"
(Patent), 42/-

LANCASTER'S "PORTABLE INSTANTOGRAPH"
(Patent), 42/-

LANCASTER'S "ROVER"
(Patent), 63/-

# J. LANCASTER & SON,
## OPTICIANS,
## BIRMINGHAM.

THE LARGEST MAKERS IN THE WORLD.

Illustrated Catalogue, Four Stamps.
Abridged List Free.

"HOW TO BE A SUCCESSFUL AMATEUR PHOTOGRAPHER."

By W. J. LANCASTER, F.C.S., &c.

POST FREE, 1s.

## The Magic Lantern

The photographs in this book are taken from magic lantern projection slides. The magic lantern was the predecessor of the pre-digital slide projector. The first ones were made in the mid-1600s by natural philosophers (early scientists) who were exploring the nature and commercial potential of optics. Light sources and lenses improved throughout the 1700s and 1800s and, as a consequence, it was possible to show bigger, brighter and clearer pictures to ever larger audiences. During Queen Victoria's reign, magic lantern shows became established as mass-media entertainment. Shows could be lavish, theatrical events with all the razzmatazz of today's TV talent contests, with multiple lanterns to produce special effects. Magic lanterns were also used in Church and village halls and educational establishments for talks and lectures and, of course, in ordinary homes for family entertainment.

Some slides gave the illusion of movement. These included colourful kaleidoscopes, children skipping, a dentist pulling teeth and a man swallowing rats as he sleeps with his mouth open …… still a favourite with children (of all ages) who attend my magic lantern shows!

In the early 1800s, magic lanterns were used to create phantasmagoria horror shows, where terrifying devils, witches and the grim reaper were conjured out of thin air, with accompanying sound effects, in suitably scary venues. These shows employed the latest technology and created sophisticated illusions to entice customers to part with their money and be scared out of their wits.

Magic lantern slides were made of glass. Early ones were hand painted and expensive to produce and buy but, from the mid-1800s, photographic images were applied to slides, mass-production followed and the magic lantern industry boomed. In its heyday, the 1890s, millions of slides were made, particularly in Britain, France and America, for entertainment, amusement, education, spiritual enlightenment and moral crusades.

In Britain, lantern slides could be purchased or hired by mail-order direct from the manufacturers or from local, high-street outlets. Photographic slides produced by the best Victorian photographers, such as those reproduced in this booklet, have pin-sharp clarity and can still make an audience gasp in surprise and delight when shown as part of my Victorian magic lantern shows.

## A final note about this book

The original guide-book, reproduced here, is over one-hundred-and-twenty years old and has various age-related issues ... marks, fading, dark patches etc. and some of the illustrations within the body of the text were poor quality even when first published. I've used today's technology, which would have seemed miraculous in the nineteenth century, to make the content as clear and legible as possible.

**Andrew Gill:** I have collected historical photographs and optical antiques for over forty years. I am a professional 'magic lantern' showman presenting Victorian slide shows and giving talks on early optical entertainments for museums, festivals, special interest groups and universities. Please visit my website '**Magic Lantern World**' at www.magiclanternist.com

My booklets and photo albums are available from Amazon, simply search for the titles below. If you've enjoyed this book, please leave a review on Amazon, as good ratings are very important to independent authors. If you're disappointed, please let me know the reason, so that I can address the issue in future editions.

**Historical travel guides**
New York
Jersey in 1921
Norwich in 1880
Doon the Watter
Liverpool in 1886
Nottingham in 1899
Bournemouth in 1914
Great Yarmouth in 1880
Victorian Walks in Surrey
The Way We Were: Bath
A Victorian Visit to Brighton
The Way We Were: Lincoln
A Victorian Visit to Hastings
A Victorian Visit to Falmouth
Newcastle upon Tyne in 1903
Victorian and Edwardian York
The Way We Were: Llandudno
A Victorian Visit to North Devon
The Way We Were: Manchester
A Victorian Guide to Birmingham
Leeds through the Magic Lantern
An Edwardian Guide to Leicester
Victorian and Edwardian Bradford
Victorian and Edwardian Sheffield

The Way We Were: North Cornwall
A Victorian Visit to Fowey and Looe
A Victorian Visit to Peel, Isle of Man
Doncaster through the Magic Lantern
The Way We Were: The Lake District
Lechlade to Oxford by Canoe in 1875
Guernsey, Sark and Alderney in 1921
East Devon through the Magic Lantern
The River Thames from Source to Sea
A Victorian Visit to Ramsey, Isle of Man
A Victorian Visit to Douglas, Isle of Man
Victorian Totnes through the Magic Lantern
Victorian Whitby through the Magic Lantern
Victorian London through the Magic Lantern
St. Ives through the Victorian Magic Lantern
Victorian Torquay through the Magic Lantern
Victorian Glasgow through the Magic Lantern
The Way We Were: Wakefield and Dewsbury
The Way We Were: Hebden Bridge to Halifax
Victorian Blackpool through the Magic Lantern
Victorian Scarborough through the Magic Lantern
The Way We Were: Hull and the Surrounding Area
The Way We Were: Harrogate and Knaresborough
A Victorian Tour of North Wales: Rhyl to Llandudno
A Victorian Visit to Lewes and the surrounding area
The Isle of Man through the Victorian Magic Lantern
A Victorian Visit to Helston and the Lizard Peninsula
A Victorian Railway Journey from Plymouth to Padstow
A Victorian Visit to Barmouth and the Surrounding Area
The Way We Were: Holmfirth, Honley and Huddersfield
A Victorian Visit to Malton, Pickering and Castle Howard
A Victorian Visit to Eastbourne and the surrounding area
A Victorian Visit to Aberystwyth and the Surrounding Area
The Way We Were: Rotherham and the Surrounding Area
A Victorian Visit to Castletown, Port St. Mary and Port Erin
Penzance and Newlyn through the Victorian Magic Lantern
A Victorian Journey to Snowdonia, Caernarfon and Pwllheli
Victorian Brixham and Dartmouth through the Magic Lantern
Victorian Plymouth and Devonport through the Magic Lantern
A Victorian Tour of North Wales: Conwy to Caernarfon via Anglesey
Staithes, Runswick and Robin Hood's Bay through the Magic Lantern
Dawlish, Teignmouth and Newton Abbot through the Victorian Magic Lantern

**Walking Books**
Victorian Edinburgh Walks
Victorian Rossendale Walks
More Victorian Rossendale Walks

Victorian Walks on the Isle of Wight (Book 1)
Victorian Walks on the Isle of Wight (Book 2)
Victorian Rossendale Walks: The End of an Era

**Other historical topics**
The YMCA in the First World War
Sarah Jane's Victorian Tour of Scotland
The River Tyne through the Magic Lantern
The 1907 Wrench Cinematograph Catalogue
Victorian Street Life through the Magic Lantern
The First World War through the Magic Lantern
Ballyclare May Fair through the Victorian Magic Lantern
The Story of Burnley's Trams through the Magic Lantern
The Franco-British 'White City' London Exhibition of 1908
The 1907 Wrench 'Optical and Science Lanterns' Catalogue
The CWS Crumpsall Biscuit Factory through the Magic Lantern
How They Built the Forth Railway Bridge: A Victorian Magic Lantern Show

**Historical photo albums (just photos)**
The Way We Were: Suffolk
Norwich: The Way We Were
The Way We Were: Somerset
Fife through the Magic Lantern
York through the Magic Lantern
Rossendale: The Way We Were
The Way We Were: Cumberland
Burnley through the Magic Lantern
Oban to the Hebrides and St. Kilda
Tasmania through the Magic Lantern
Swaledale through the Magic Lantern
Llandudno through the Magic Lantern
Birmingham through the Magic Lantern
Penzance, Newlyn and the Isles of Scilly
Great Yarmouth through the Magic Lantern
Ancient Baalbec through the Magic Lantern
The Isle of Skye through the Magic Lantern
Ancient Palmyra through the Magic Lantern
The Kentish Coast from Whitstable to Hythe
New South Wales through the Magic Lantern
From Glasgow to Rothesay by Paddle Steamer
Victorian Childhood through the Magic Lantern
The Way We Were: Yorkshire Railway Stations
Southampton, Portsmouth and the Great Liners
Newcastle upon Tyne through the Magic Lantern
Egypt's Ancient Monuments through the Magic Lantern
The Way We Were: Birkenhead, Port Sunlight and the Wirral
Ancient Egypt, Baalbec and Palmyra through the Magic Lantern

Copyright © 2021 by Andrew Gill. All rights reserved.
No part of this book may be reproduced or used in any
manner without written permission of the copyright owner.

Contact email: victorianhistory@virginmedia.com

Printed in Great Britain
by Amazon